# CDL
# MINDED
# INVE$TOR

## HAVE UNLIMITED INCOME, BUILD PASSIVE CASH FLOW, AND GAIN INFINITE RETURNS FOR LONG-TERM WEALTH IN TRANSPORTATION AND TRUCKING BUSINESS INDUSTRY

# JOE RYDER

# CONTENTS

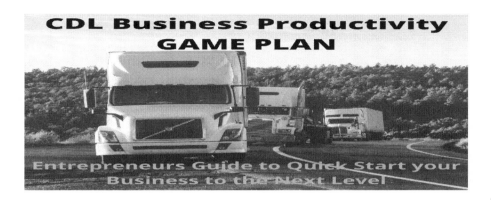

Thank you! Here's a Free Gift! For You :)

As a special thanks from me to you, you'll receive:

- ❑ 3 Powerful Elements of Productivity in your Business
- ❑ 5 Simple Strategies to Mastering Productivity in your Business
- ❑ The Highest Quality of Productivity Charts
- ❑ Valuable Resources that you Must Know and much more!

To receive your Free copy of the CDL Business Productivity
GAME PLAN, you can go to my website at:

cdlforlife.com/cdl-business-resources

<u>SCAN ME</u>
(For your Free Business Game Plan)

<u>SCAN ME</u>
(If you want my Books for Free)

Also If you would like to get my books for Free and
before anyone else, go to my website at:

cdlforlife.com/cdl-business-resources

# INTRODUCTION

*I will tell you how to become rich.*
*Close the door. Be careful when others are greedy.*
*Be greedy when others are careful*

—Warren Buffet

After more than 25 years in the trucking industry, seeing drivers and companies alike come and go, and after hauling tons of cargo and driving for what seems like a lifetime, I can speak on both sides of this business and on the opportunities for success or failures within the industry. This, whether you're a beginner looking to make some extra money or a veteran that's looking to expand your business to the next level. In this industry, you can make consistent income without the pain, struggle and hassle that most people go through. By having the right plan in place, you can avoid the common mistakes that most people make when investing in any business. I will reveal some industry secrets to you like how to have a healthy cash flow, how to have a positive Return on Investment (ROI) and how to have a large net profit that will build, grow and sustain your business for the long haul.

You have the potential to not only make big bucks from the trucking industry but to also make passive and consistent income without necessarily having to start a trucking business. In CDL Minded Investor, I'll unveil the entrepreneur secrets to financial freedom by understanding and applying the helpful strategies and tips shared here. By tapping into the opportunities in the trucking business, you can take full advantage of what this industry has to offer.

Truck drivers are some of the unsung heroes of our economic progress and as the country grows from one economic milestone to the next, truck drivers work silently behind the scenes, making sure that everyone gets what they need when they need it. Truck drivers are the reason why you go to your favorite supermarket and find it fully stocked. They are the reason why most organizations are fully operational because all the supplies they need are delivered on time.

On a smaller scale, you may not see the impact of truck drivers. However, when you broaden your perspective and look at the bigger picture, the trucking and transportation industry is simply the main reason why most of us are able to get on with life every day. The trucking industry is the glue that holds supply chains in most industries together.

At a personal level, trucking is an incredible investment opportunity. In a world where many people have had to rethink their career paths since the 2020 Covid-19 pandemic, investing in this sector is actually a great idea. Today, many people are excited about the prospect of creating passive income streams. This is a smart financial move, because most of the time, you simply need to manage the business, while someone else does the active duties. You can get into the trucking business as a driver, or own the business and create employment opportunities for other enterprising individuals. Such is the kind of flexibility that you will enjoy in this industry.

One of the first things you are always advised to do before getting into any business is to research the sector well enough. Well, the same applies to the trucking industry. Research helps you understand how the industry works, whether there are opportunities you can tap into, and most importantly, the opportunities for growth. It would be pointless to invest your money in an industry that cannot grow.

Now, if you conduct your research well, you won't miss the general concern that the trucking industry has had a shortage of truck drivers for years. That right there is a good starting point. Having a shortage of drivers easily translates to there being a huge demand for drivers. Growth in the trucking industry is generally directly proportional to the increasing demands of consumers in different sectors. Players in those sectors must adapt and adjust their supply chains to ensure that they can still deliver on time and cater to the needs of their customers. Unfortunately, the trucking industry has been lagging behind in terms of recruitment, hence the persistent shortage that has plagued the industry for years.

On the bright side, this is positive for beginners, as well as for current investors, because you are almost certain to hit the ground running and make a fortune in the CDL (Commercial Driver's License) trucking industry. That is the core foundation of what this book is about.

I was once in your position, a beginner in the trucking industry. Over the years, I've also come across many beginners, who I mentored from my experience, and some went on to become close friends that I even consider my trucking family.

I understand your key pain points because I have been there. Someone held my hand and ushered me into the business, and it's only right that I pass down my knowledge and experience to help you too.

You may feel a bit frustrated that you don't have your CDL yet, and the formalities may be a pain, but that shouldn't break your spirit. These are normal industry procedures that you'd expect in any other sector.

You may even be skilled in other aspects of running a business, but when it comes to trucking, it feels like a different game altogether. Well, don't throw away your business knowledge yet. There's so much you can borrow from that knowledge that will make it easier for you to find your footing in trucking. This, after all, is an investment, and most, if not all, investment principles will be relevant.

You're probably also worried about the amount of money you'll need to get into this business. Trust me, it's not as much as you may think it is. This is one of the huge stumbling blocks that first-timers in the trucking industry worry about, but as you read on, you'll realize that you were probably more ready to invest in the trucking industry than you thought you were. That's the thing about life in general. We waste a lot of time waiting for the right moment to do something great, not realizing that we were ready all along.

I have always loved the beautiful sound of a roaring engine, watching countless shooting stars, catching lots of sunrises, and the freedom that comes with being on the open road. This is how I knew trucking was my calling. Your story may not be similar to mine, but if there's one thing I can guarantee you, it's that once you get into the trucking business and figure your way around it, you'll wonder why you didn't start sooner.

Finally, as you take your first steps in the trucking industry, always remember that experience will get you places, and everyone started from somewhere. This is more than an exciting career; it's an opportunity for job security and the freedom to choose your career path. You must be intentional in your approach, commit yourself, and put in the effort. This is an investment opportunity of a lifetime. With the lessons you'll get from this book, you are already on your way to an amazing future as a CDL Minded Investor.

# CHAPTER 1

# CULTIVATING THE MINDSET FOR SUCCESS

**N**avigating the world of business isn't one of the easiest things to do. There are actually grim statistics suggesting that many new and upcoming businesses face struggles. Yet, at the same time, many businesses defy the odds and come up on top. For medium-sized and large businesses, this may come down to astute management. However, when it comes to small businesses, and in particular, sole proprietorships, there's more to success than astute management. Success or failure, in this case, is a personal affair.

Let's take a walk down memory lane to a time when you endured a significant setback in life. Perhaps it was something personal, a business loss, or anything else you can think of. Remember that low, sunken feeling? The despair, wishing you'd have, perhaps, done things differently? Amidst the flurry of emotions, you may even have felt trapped or constrained by the circumstances.

But, there's more to this...

How did you eventually get back on your feet? Herein lies the secret to unlocking success beyond your wildest imagination. In life, and in particular, when running a business, things won't always go according to plan. You actually buy insurance policies for this very reason.

How do you keep moving towards your goals, despite the heartbreak, the disappointments, and the failures? How is it that while some people may get stuck in the bad experiences, some emerge stronger, braver, and ready to challenge everything the universe throws at them? The answer is pretty simple—Attitude!

The simplest definition of attitude is your strongest feeling or thought about something. The right attitude is more often the difference between succumbing to the weight of your adversities, or overcoming them. It is how you tackle your problems, push your limits and achieve your goals.

The right attitude can help you push beyond your inhibitions, break free of your doubts and conquer your world. A positive attitude is such a powerful and transformative force because it not only reshapes your state of mind, it also helps you become a better person, mentally, emotionally and physically.

The right attitude is a mandatory prerequisite for success—any kind of success. This is true because success never comes easy. You'll have to rise above unique challenges every day, come up with innovative strategies to create a winning template for success. Many of the renowned investors we read about overcame challenges that would make most people give up today. Yet their motivation, determination, and inspiration never wavered, not even at their most trying moments. There's so much we can learn from their experiences.

The trucking, transportation and logistics industry has always been a hot topic for new investors looking to grow some passive income, and rightly so. This industry is the backbone of the economy. Everything you use was a consignment at some point in the wider supply chain. Therefore, as you prepare to get into this industry in the hope that you can enjoy vast success and build your empire, you must be careful not to ignore the lurking risks, as much as you are excited about the potential profits.

This is one industry where you have as much a likelihood of success as failure. We read about successful truckers who have built their empire over the years, while at the same time, we also read about those who swear never to get into this industry again. Well, the reasons behind either of these scenarios may vary, so let's narrow it down to one reason that is fully within your control—YOU!

It's time to invest in the CDL Trucking and Transportation industry and enjoy all of the wealth and freedom that comes with it. You will face some challenges, but if you are really committed to improving your quality of life, you won't let that hold you back. When you start thinking about the road ahead as an exciting new opportunity, you'll soon find that all of the challenges were worth the amazing results. If you want to run a successful business that ensures you'll never have to miss out on family time or worry about your financial situation again, you need to become a CDL Minded Investor.

## Optimizing Investments

How do you create that winning mindset? How do you use it to turn simple business decisions into smart investment decisions? How do you stay focused even when everything is stacked against you?

The success you seek is all in your mind. It's only once you conquer your mind that you can rise to the next level and make decisions that improve your financial outlook. No one is born a successful investor. It takes a lot of learning, mistakes, difficult decisions, and time to get there. More importantly, there's a lot of planning that goes into becoming a successful investor.

Every business opportunity carries some level of risk. It doesn't matter whether this is your first attempt at business or you have years of experience. Risk is always imminent. Your goal is to make plans to completely avert the risk, or if that's not possible, significantly reduce the impact it may have on your investment.

So, how do you become THAT person?

Your first priority is to make yourself the priority. You'd be surprised at the way we take good health for granted. Most people just breeze through life without thinking about what it means to actually care for themselves. It's the simple things like resting, hydrating, getting enough sleep, and eating well that keep you going. Business demands can take a toll on you. It gets worse if you don't give much attention to your overall wellness.

Next, you should understand your thought process. What drives you to make the big decisions? Are you the kind of person who goes against the grain most of the time, or do you follow a strict code? Do you bow down to societal pressure? Are your decisions biased? These are important considerations that help you understand the motivations behind your decisions. These influences are your reality, so it would be wise to learn what pushes you a certain way.

Now that you have some understanding of what works for you, let's segue into the business idea. Why do you want to invest in the trucking and logistics sector? There may be other business opportunities of interest, so why this one? What criteria did you use to leave out alternatives from your list and settle on this industry?

How sustainable is the idea? The trucking business, for example, has stood the test of time, thanks to its pivotal function in our lives. Trucking pretty much is the backbone of every industry. Technological advancements have made the sector more efficient over time, but its role in the economic value chain has never changed.

Most people want to become successful entrepreneurs at some point, but not everyone is cut out for it. Entrepreneurship comes with its unique challenges, and without the mettle for it, you may bow out at the first sign of struggle. We already know that losses are a normal part of the business. However, the question you should answer is how much loss is too much for you? This is how you know when to cut your losses and try something else, or stick your neck out for the business and ride out the storm. This is an important consideration that helps to prepare you mentally for potential challenges in the business.

Building on the mental preparedness point above, there's no better way to optimize your investment in a business than enhancing your understanding of it. How well do you know the business? The trucking industry, for example, is one with lots of moving parts. Take your time and study all the crucial determinants in the industry. What factors are within your control and which ones aren't? Know how local, national, regional, or even global politics may affect your business. How do factors beyond your control, like the weather, affect your margins?

Finally, you are now a business owner. It doesn't matter whether it's your first day in the business or three years down the line, you must learn to conduct yourself like a business owner. One of your core tasks as a business owner is to create value in your brand. How do you grow the business? How do you make it the perfect place for your employees to work? Employees are your brand ambassadors. You have to create an ideal working environment that enables them to deliver on their promise to you.

## Developing a Winning Mindset

The most important, and probably the most powerful, tool you have is your mindset. Once you put your mind to something and are committed to it, nothing can stand in your way. This is how some people become consistent winners in almost every venture they channel their attention to. A winning mindset gives you the confidence to pursue opportunities that other people would not. You see opportunities where others see challenges and obstacles. You don't give in to failure because you understand the lessons that you're learning from, and growing from them plays a crucial role to your success.

One of the best things about developing a winning mindset is multifaceted growth, both in your professional and personal life. So much time and effort goes into building wealth, and to achieve it all, your mindset must align with your goals. How do you get from where you are to a winning mindset? Here are some important traits you must have:

## 1. Self-Awareness

The first step is to answer an important question—what do you want? Now there are as many answers to this question as you can imagine, most of which are correct. The challenge is how to prioritize the correctness of the answers with respect to developing a winning mindset.

If you don't know what you're working towards, how will you ever achieve it?

If you don't know what you are looking for, how will you know when you find it?

Once you become aware of what you seek, you become confident and determined to pursue it. There are many things you can do to become better at something, but none of that will matter if you don't know what the end result is.

Be clear in your goals. For example, you want to develop a winning mindset. How do you approach this?

There's a lot of learning involved. The internet allows you access to millions of pieces of enriching content from people who have achieved great things. From books and interviews, to webinars and videos, you name it, it's available. You can learn from their exploits as much as their struggles. This opens your eyes and helps you realize that if you push yourself just a little bit, you can have the whole world in the palm of your hands.

## 2. Focus

It's easier said than done.

Like what you want, focus is another vast concept. You may even be tempted to ask: focus on what?

But what you need isn't to dwell on the act of concentrating on something, but instead, how to create that habit. It's the subtle, simple things you do that help you learn how to focus. For example, start waking up early every day and make it a habit. You may not realize it at first, but shifting your wake-up time, say two or three hours before your normal day begins, changes your mental dimension. Use this time to do one or two things that can improve your life. There's so much you can do with that extra time. You can read, or meditate. Some quiet time, especially just before your busy day begins, can help you sharpen your thoughts.

Here's another thing you can work into your schedule—exercise! You probably knew about that already. But the immense benefits of regular exercise, especially early in the morning, have been widely documented over the years. Take a walk, jog a bit, ride a bike. If you can score at least half an hour of aerobics every morning, you're doing better than most. Besides, your heart will thank you for it!

## 3. Grow Up!

Have you ever spent time with colleagues, peers, or any other adult who never seemed to find fault in their ways? In their world, it's always someone else's fault. Now, this may be describing someone else, or yourself, but the truth is that you must learn to take responsibility for your choices and actions if you are to become a winner.

People make mistakes all the time. We already mentioned that you must be willing to learn from your mistakes, so that you can improve and become a better person. Being a responsible adult is one of the most important aspects of growing up, and people around you will respect you for it.

This isn't just about admitting that you are wrong or that you made a mistake, it's mostly about being honest with yourself, especially when no one is watching. If you assess your strengths and weaknesses, you can identify some crucial areas where you can improve and become a better person.

## 4. Shun the Herd Mentality

A winning mindset means learning how to lead. Instead of following the crowd, be the light that guides them. To achieve this, you must shun all forms of mediocrity and stop settling for the average life. There may be times when people will doubt you. Your vision may not be clear to them just yet. However, since you already know what you are working on, and what lies on the other side of your effort, keep going. The fruits of your craziness will become apparent in due course, and they'll label you a genius.

Taking the easy route can only yield average results. You are better than that. Don't concern yourself with what other people are doing. Focus on your race and run it. Usually, shifting your attention to what others are doing can only breed distractions, so stay focused and stay in your lane.

## 5. Be Persistent

You don't just wake up one day and become a winner. The winning mindset takes a lot of consistent effort and persistence. No one will hand you anything on a silver platter, especially something that leads to greatness. Doors may be slammed on your face, but those aren't the only doors available. Opportunities will always exist, so even if you lose one or a few, there will be more tomorrow.

Persistence and consistency go hand in hand. Even with the weight of the world on your shoulders, show up and do the work. They say the darkest hour is before the dawn. Resist that urge to cave in and quit. Remember, you are in this with the long-term in mind, so stay the course.

One of the best things about persistence, especially when it seems everything is stacked against you, is that you eventually learn how to adapt to overcome challenges, and you also become creative at finding solutions. Using this approach, you will have endless possibilities and opportunities at every turn. Get out of your comfort zone and push your limits.

You must also be consistent in taking care of the most important factor of success—YOU! Eat well; get enough exercise, hydrate and sleep well. You can't be working hard at everything else but yourself. A healthy body gives your mind all the ammunition you need to do the unthinkable, a crucial factor in becoming a risk taker.

Ultimately, opportunities don't always come to everyone. Even so, many people don't realize what they have until it's long gone. Besides, there aren't enough opportunities for everyone anyway. Take your chances, seize the moment and be the embodiment of the greatness you've always dreamt of. A mindset change is the ultimate lifestyle change, and it's only a matter of time until the results unfold before your eyes.

## Getting Your Ambitions Right

Success isn't a sprint. It's a marathon, and the right mindset and attitude only gets you halfway through it. Now, the remaining half once again comes down to how far you are willing to push yourself. It's about your ambition. How much do you really want to succeed?

When we talk about ambition, we must also be careful not to detach ourselves from the realities of life. While it's good to be ambitious, it's even better if you're working on tangible future prospects. You must be aware of the opportunities and limitations unique to your present circumstances in life and work around them diligently. Therefore, your ambition must also be reasonably practical.

Here are some simple questions to guide you:

## 1. Do I really want this?

This is purely about making sure your mind is in the right place. Set goals that you are passionate about. For example, a lot of people are excited about the prospect of succeeding in the trucking industry, but not all of them are passionate about it.

Being passionate about something gives you the belief that you can achieve it. It also keeps you motivated, especially during the difficult periods that every business goes through from time to time.

## 2. Are my goals achievable?

Achievability is all about practicality and working towards goals that are reasonable. This keeps you grounded, knowing that you will eventually succeed. Don't just choose something that's easy to achieve. You need a challenge that's reasonably complex in order to sharpen your skills and push you out of your comfort zone.

## 3. How do I go about it?

You'll mostly have multiple goals to achieve when running a successful business. The question for you is, how do you achieve all of them without ever running into conflict? This comes down to creating an elaborate action plan and figuring out your priorities. You must focus and give your best effort to each of your goals. Work on them one at a time while taking note of the milestones as you go.

## 4. When will I see the results?

Your ambitious plan must come to fruition at some point. Therefore, this is all about setting deadlines. Clear deadlines give you the extra push to work smarter and achieve your goals by a certain time. Deadlines can also be great evaluation tools that will help you adjust your timelines for future projects accordingly.

## 5. What if things don't work out?

Now, things won't always go according to plan, and that's okay. When this happens, you must stay positive and look to the future. If you fail, take it as a stepping stone and learn from it. While you may realize some expected results right away, some may take longer, but if you do things right, everything will be okay.

Lessons aren't only available in the losses and mistakes, but in your wins too. Once you achieve your goals, go back to the drawing board and retrace your steps. How did you do it? What was the height of your accomplishment? At what point did you almost give up? What did you learn from that experience, and how can you use it to help you in similar projects going forward?

Success is an ongoing process of results and evaluation. Once you are set on the right path, there's no turning back. You can only get better and do better. Ultimately, the right investment decisions come down to having the right mindset, executing your action plan, and confidently pursuing your targets.

## Checklist and CDL Minded Approach

Cultivating the right mindset to run a trucking and transportation business isn't something that happens overnight. As you proceed and learn more about the industry, you should continuously assess yourself and find ways of improving your thought process. This is what makes successful entrepreneurs different from everyone else.

Follow this checklist to assess your self-awareness with respect to the demands of your investment, and push your limits to become a successful entrepreneur in the trucking industry:

| Crucial goals for the week | Tasks involved | Did you accomplish them? Yes or no. If yes, what did you do to complete this task? If not, what stopped you from achieving it? |
|---|---|---|
| Routine exercises for a healthy body | Anything to get you moving, like running, jogging, going to the gym. | |
| Create work schedules | Plan your week in advance. Schedule meetings, projects, and tasks. | |
| Manage deadlines | Highlight all your deadlines for the week, and prioritize them accordingly. | |
| Backup plans | Review your schedules and deadlines, and note tasks that may require a backup plan if things don't go according to plan. | |

# CHAPTER 2

# THE PRELIMINARY INVESTMENT DRILL

When you're getting into the world of business, you hope that your decisions will be good investment decisions. Good and wise investment decisions are those that align with your personal goals and objectives and, more importantly, match your risk appetite. Everyone hopes to make the right investment decisions. However, the challenge comes in figuring out the right place to invest their money. Without the right approach to investment, you may make some money, but end up losing more than you anticipated in the process. So, how can you make sure you do it right? Well, that's what this chapter is about. Read on to learn how to get started, understand your risk exposure, and how to avoid some simple, yet common mistakes most people make.

## Understanding Good Investments

There are lots of investment opportunities in the CDL industry. Like every other investment market, these opportunities exist in different forms and shapes, and ultimately are the backbone of the economy. A good investment is one that not only helps you make money but also gives a great return on your investment. If we take a wider perspective, it is one that becomes a consistent and reliable opportunity for creating long-term wealth actively, passively and residually.

Utilizing the investment opportunities that come your way is one of the most reliable approaches to financial independence. The truth is, many people hope they can make just enough money to retire early and enjoy a peaceful life but they never achieve it. Unfortunately, most of them approach this by saving. While a saving culture is a good thing, it's not entirely enough to earn you that quiet and peaceful retirement life you seek. Saving carries little risk, and you may even lose money through inflation if you solely use this approach.

Investment is the only way to truly achieve most, if not all, of your financial goals. This is because investment takes into account something that saving doesn't—risk! At all times, always strive to ensure that your investment decisions are guided not only by your goals and objectives, but mostly by your risk appetite.

So, assuming that you have all those in place, what really makes an investment good, or better than others?

We've already mentioned your goals and risk appetite. Other factors that may make an investment worthwhile include having the appropriate budget for it, and whether there's potential for growth in that opportunity.

On the face of it, it's impossible to tell whether an investment will be worth your while. However, there are some good indicators you can use to determine whether an opportunity is worth putting your money into, and more importantly, if it will be a valuable investment over time. Let's look at some of them below:

## 1. Reliable Income Potential

A good investment should be capable of delivering consistent income throughout its lifetime. Take a moment and think about the CDL industry's performance over the years. Even during the Covid-19 pandemic, when most industries ground to a halt, the need for trucking was more important than ever.

This is an industry that defies the odds during harsh economic conditions because it props up every other sector of the economy. In terms of consistent revenue, the CDL trucking sector checks that box, whether the economy is thriving or not.

## 2. Competitive Edge

What's so unique about this sector that gives it an advantage over other opportunities? First, we have to ask ourselves, who are the competitors? In this sector, your competition is other truckers and any other businesses within the wider transport, trucking and logistics sector. What's so unique about this opportunity that can make it survive market volatility and pressure from other competing businesses? There's got to be something about this opportunity that makes you want to invest in it, despite the fact that there are many other truckers already in the business.

## 3. Debt Management

How much debt are you working with? There are many investments that may seem like amazing opportunities at a glance, but once you study the finer details, you realize that they are not really worth your time and money. It's unfortunate that many new investors barely consider debt, perhaps because they don't know how to go about it.

While debt generally isn't a bad thing, you should be careful not to take on too much of it. It would not be a wise investment decision to immediately be crippled by debt when you start the business. A better approach to debt is to figure out whether you can afford to pay it off comfortably without hurting the growth potential of your business.

## 4. Passive Income Potential

The ultimate goal when setting up a business opportunity is to turn it into a reliable source of passive income. Unfortunately, not all investment opportunities can deliver on this promise. The concept of passive income hinges on the fact that you must not be actively involved in running the business. Depending on how you handle it, the trucking industry can be an incredible and reliable source of passive income. People have done it before, and you can do it as well.

## 5. True Value

What's the real cost of setting up that investment opportunity? Now, from time to time, you'll come across an investment that meets all the indicators we've discussed above, and assume that it's the right call to put your money in it. Before you do that, however, you need to understand all the costs involved in setting up and managing that opportunity.

The true value, in this case, is primarily about getting a fair market value for your money. Remember that the point of investing, as we've seen in the discussions above, is to not just make money, but revenue so reliable that it becomes a source of passive income. Weigh all the costs involved in setting up the business to determine whether the opportunity is overvalued or not.

Pouring your money into an overvalued investment is unwise because it may take you longer than you anticipated to break even and start turning profits. An overvalued investment eats into your potential earnings, so you'd be making losses masked as profits.

This is where due diligence comes in. Research well any opportunity to understand not just the business, but more importantly, the dynamics of the overall market and industry. This gives you a better perspective of what you are getting into, and if your planned budget is appropriate.

## Low-Risk Versus High-Risk Investments

In simple terms, risk is the possibility of something bad happening. For your investment, this translates to the possibility of losing your money. As grim as the picture may sound, risk is actually a fundamental aspect of every investment, which you must always be aware of. Given that there are no distinct measurements of risk, your awareness and understanding of the risk involved in an investment opportunity can greatly reduce your chances of losing all your money.

There are two types of investments—high-risk investments and low-risk investments. A high-risk investment is one where there's a very high likelihood of underperformance, or that you'll lose your money. Interestingly enough, these are also the investments that, if successful, have the highest potential for massive earnings.

Low-risk investments are the exact opposite. In such cases, you have less to worry about, as there's a very slim chance that the investment may underperform. Apart from that, such investments also mean that even if you were to suffer a loss, the impact would not be devastating. As you can imagine, these investments generally have a low return potential compared to high-risk investments.

While the general consensus is that low risks have lower returns and high risks have higher returns, this is only a guideline and it's not necessarily set in stone. This is why it's important to not just assume the level of risk when considering an investment, but to understand the nature of the risk. For example, if a business has too much debt, it's generally a high-risk investment. This doesn't mean that it will deliver high returns. If anything, there's a higher chance of default in this case. Naturally, businesses with low debt tend to deliver better returns over the long term because they have fewer entities laying claim to their profits.

## Volatility as a Measure of Risk

We've already mentioned that risk is crucial to investment. The challenge for first-time investors is usually trying to understand not just the difference between low and high risk, but also to figure out where the risk might occur. This happens because the risk is neither easily quantifiable, nor properly defined, so it's almost impossible to agree on an exact way of measuring it either.

Often, people use volatility as a means of measuring risk. Volatility tells you how much a given value may vary over time. For example, there's a high chance that some possibilities will be unfavorable if you have a wide range of possibilities to choose from. This is why volatility is considered a fairly easy measure of risk to understand. However, it still doesn't capture the true picture of risk in an investment.

A volatile investment generally means that as an investor, you are exposed to a higher possibility of different outcomes. What you may not realize, however, is that there's no proof that any of those outcomes will happen. This is a major flaw of volatility as a measure of risk. It's like driving on a bumpy road. The experience isn't pleasant, but it doesn't necessarily mean that you'll have an accident.

## Evaluating Risk Preference

From our discussion above, it's important to learn how to figure out the right amount of risk you can take in any investment. People have different levels of risk tolerance; therefore it's impossible to come up with a strategy that cuts across the board. To make your work easier, however, you need to consider two important factors: time and your investment value.

Regarding time, the question you need to answer is how long are you willing to keep your money tied up in the investment?

If you need to invest $20,000, but will need to use that money in a few months for an urgent need, like college tuition, or for a down payment on a house, your best approach is to consider low-risk investments. This is because there's a relatively low chance of price fluctuation within such a short time. If you intend to use the money in maybe ten years, you can consider higher-risk investments.

The reasoning here is that a longer duration allows your investment sufficient time to bounce back, whereas a shorter duration may not. Therefore, if you buy, for example, stock in a company, ten years is sufficient time for the stock to go through the full economic cycle, where it may lose value at some point, and rally back and even higher.

On your investment value, risk tolerance is about how much money you are willing to lose in the event that things don't work out. It doesn't sound like such a positive outlook, but it is a realistic approach. As a rule of thumb, people are often advised to invest only the amount of money that they can afford to lose, or forgo for a given period of time.

This concept helps you get on with life, regardless of what happens to your investment. For example, you may have $20,000 to invest, but are only comfortable investing $16,000. In that case, only invest the $16,000 so that your life doesn't stop in case of any unforeseen circumstances.

Naturally, the more money you have to invest, the bigger the risks you are willing to take. Further, if you have $2 million and another person has $20,000, and you both invest $16,000, the investor with $2 million will be the least worried if the investment declines in value over time.

## *Compounding and Your Money*

Compounding is a common investment concept you'll come across from time to time. It implies the potential of your investment to generate income which is subsequently reinvested, generating even more earnings. In simpler terms, compounding means earning from income you already earned.

There are three important factors that make compounding possible—that you reinvest your money, the duration of time your money is invested, and the amount of money you invested in the first place. These three are crucial aspects of investment, as wealth builders, which we'll also discuss in the next chapter.

Let's explain compounding with a simple example:

Say you invest $20,000 in a trucking business. At the end of the first year, your investment earns 12%. It is now worth $22,400. Since the business is performing well, you reinvest the full amount, and in the second year, it still earns 12%. At this point, your $22,400 is now worth $25,008.

The difference here is that instead of the 12% growth earning you $2,400 as in the first year, it's earned you an extra $208, simply because the profit you earned in the first year is also earning income.

If you keep your money invested, you'll keep earning profits every year, and as your profits keep growing, so does the potential for your investment. It gets even better when you invest additional money into the business.

Compounding can be done annually, semiannually, quarterly, or even monthly. The more compounding periods you have in a year, the higher your income earnings. For example, monthly compounding means your money will be growing every month. Any amount earned as interest immediately starts earning you interest on itself. That's how compounding works.

From our previous example, you can also understand how the other two factors (duration of time and amount invested) come into play. Investing a lot of money for a longer duration accelerates the earning potential of your initial investment. Let's say you invested $20,000 consistently, earning 12% every year for five years. At the end of this period, your money will have grown to $35,247. On the other hand, if you invested for seven years, you'd have $44,214, and $62,117 if you invested for ten years. See how the aspect of time works?

Now, apart from the discussions above, there are some special considerations that may affect the risk profile of your investment, which you should consider when evaluating risk. Even if you put your money in an investment that you can mostly consider a safe investment, there's always a risk of that business failing. Good examples here are Enron and Lehman Brothers Holdings Inc. These were once successful enterprises that many investors considered a sure win for their portfolios, yet they eventually collapsed.

It's advisable, therefore, not to put all your money in one place, especially when you consider the risk of market volatility. Even if you have every reason to believe that an investment is safe, you should still diversify and spread your money into other investments. This reduces the risk of your entire investment portfolio underperforming and collapsing.

Another potential for significant loss is creating a portfolio of low-risk investments, which all share the same kind of risk. For example, investing only in treasury bonds. Of course, the risk in treasury bonds is low, but they all share the same type of risk. So, if something happens that affects the treasury bonds market, like the government defaulting on its promise to pay the bonds, your entire investment would fail.

## Common Mistakes Most Beginners Make

People make mistakes all the time. However, when you start a business, making fewer mistakes increases your chances of enjoying better returns on your investment. Since you cannot avoid mistakes all the time, the best you can do is learn from other people's experiences and make smarter, better decisions. Here are some common beginner mistakes that you can avoid:

- No Investment Plan

Simply put, failing to plan is the easiest way of planning to fail. Without an investment plan, you clearly have no idea what you are doing. An investment plan guides you on important decisions like staffing, growth, and financing. Always make sure you have a solid investment plan, and review it regularly to make sure it still serves your needs.

- Chasing After Performance

Some investment classes may be quite profitable at the moment, making them look like exciting opportunities. However, what you may not realize is that the perfect opportunity to invest in them may have been a year or two ago. Don't just buy into the hype of an investment. Study it well and understand the factors behind its performance, then make a wise decision.

- Investing with a Trader Mindset

Traders aim for short-term gains, while investors put their money in for the long-term. A trader can buy an asset in the morning and sell it in the afternoon to take advantage of slight price fluctuations. An investor, on the other hand, looks at the bigger picture, and invests with a long-term vision.

- Getting Too Emotional

One of the most important things about investing in any business is that you should never be emotionally involved. It's normal for businesses to go through difficult times, but if you are emotionally involved, you'll struggle during these times. It's not just the business you need to detach your emotions from, you must also detach emotions from the numbers. Don't be too obsessed with how much you earn or how much you lost.

- Investing on Recommendations

While it's a good idea to listen to people's recommendations about viable investments, that should never be the basis of your investment actions. Listen to recommendations, but do your own research.

- Copying Others

Do not follow other investors blindly. People make investment decisions based on what is right for them at that particular time. If you follow the herd, you may end up chasing after hot investments whose momentum may have already died, and are on the verge of a decline.

- Ignoring Risk Aversion

Before you invest, try to learn the imminent risks, and whether you can afford to take them. Your appetite for risk should guide you, such that you don't take on more risk than you can handle. It's okay to ignore an investment that everyone is excited about, simply because it feels like too much risk for you, rather than to flow with the trend and risk losing everything.

- Forgetting Time Horizon

Earlier on, we discussed the importance of the time factor in your investments. The longer you invest, the better your prospects in terms of compounding. Some investments are only good opportunities when you get in at the right time. Otherwise, you may not make so much from them, or even lose everything when you invest at the wrong time. Therefore, don't just look at whether the investment is good for you or not, find out if the timing is right.

- Letting Losses Grow

Even though losses are normal in business, letting them grow and get out of hand is utter carelessness. Investigate the source of your losses and come up with a plan to bounce back. Even if the entire industry or economy is going through a rough time, this doesn't mean you rest and assume that things will pick up on their own. You are the champion of change, so create the changes you want.

- Lack of Diversity

This is the age-old problem of keeping all your eggs in one basket. Even though it is a widely discussed problem among beginner investors, people still make this mistake. Don't put all your money in one investment. Your money is safer when you spread it around into assets with varying risk profiles.

- Insufficient Research

As a beginner, one thing is certain—that you don't really understand the market like an expert does. You may know about the prices, but have no knowledge of other crucial factors like seasonal trends, patterns, and other industry-specific data. If you're excited about an investment, take your time and learn as much as you can about it. This will help you understand not just the investment, but the dynamics of making money with it.

Ultimately, investment is all about knowing where and when to put your money, and when to take it out. If you can do that, you'll definitely have a better chance of growing your wealth. This is why it's wise to avoid the common beginner mistakes, so you don't fall into the same trap.

## Checklist and CDL Minded Approach

One of the most important things in any investment is learning the type of investor you are. As there are low and high-risk types of investments, it's also important to understand the kind of risk-taker you are. Figuring this out will help you learn how to make crucial decisions without taking on more risk than you can handle.

The checklist below can help you understand the kind of investor you are. Note that it's common to exhibit characteristics of more than one type, generally depending on the type of investment. However, you'll mostly use one investment type as your fallback plan.

Below is a checklist you can use from time to time to assess your self-awareness with respect to the demands of your investment, and push your limits to become a successful entrepreneur in the trucking industry:

| Investor Type | Descriptive features | Which one describes you, and what makes you this type of an investor? |
|---|---|---|
| Risk Seeker | Your investment style is to chase the thrill and excitement of new opportunities.<br><br>Your portfolio isn't heavily diversified.<br><br>You don't research opportunities a lot, but make snap investment decisions without worrying about consequences. | |
| Risk Manager | You are extremely confident about your investments because you research well and are well informed about the market. | |

| Risk Avoider | You seek complete guarantees about returns before investing your money.<br><br>You'd rather receive a small return on your investment than risk losing everything in pursuit of a higher return.<br><br>You don't research too much, but consider assurances on safe investments from people you know and trust. | |
| --- | --- | --- |
| Risk Mitigator | You investigate investment opportunities thoroughly.<br><br>Your portfolio is heavily diversified.<br><br>You are deeply concerned about fluctuations in the market. | |

# CHAPTER 3

# GETTING INTO THE CDL INVESTMENTS

At this point, you have a rough idea of what it takes to set up a successful investment in the CDL trucking industry. You've learned the important lessons like common beginner mistakes you should avoid, and how to identify low and high-risk investments. We now go a notch higher and prepare you for the investment of a lifetime by learning the ins and outs of the trucking industry.

It's clear so far that the CDL trucking business is a good investment opportunity, primarily because every sector of the economy depends on it. It doesn't matter whether we are grappling with lockdowns and restricted movement because of a pandemic or not, truckers will always be needed to keep the country running. That's how important your business is to the economy.

In terms of value, the trucking sector injects billions of dollars into the US economy. To be precise, various reports estimate the industry turned annual returns of more than $700 billion in 2019 and 2020. As the economy keeps growing, it won't be long before the trucking industry is a trillion-dollar sector. Wouldn't it be awesome knowing that you have a role to play in that?

People have made millions in this industry by starting CDL trucking businesses and managing them successfully. It's all about recognizing the opportunities around you and maximizing their potential. In an industry that employs roughly 5% of the national workforce, there are lots of opportunities in there that you, too, can exploit to count yourself among those who make millions from CDL trucking.

## Industry Insights

We've already cast a glance at the viability of the trucking business, but do you ever wonder just exactly how big the industry is? Well, let's dig deeper into that.

Did you know that at an average of $700 billion a year, the annual earnings from the trucking industry in the US alone is worth as much, or more than, the annual GDP of more than 100 countries in the world? That's right. You could actually run several economies from the annual proceeds of the trucking industry. These statistics are the product of the hard, diligent work of close to a million truckers in the country, yet most of these truckers are contracted on minimum wages.

So how do they do it? Well, the simple answer is more than just hard and diligent work; it's about in-depth knowledge of the trucking business and the industry in general. Take the case of big retailers like Walmart as an example. They understand that to serve their customers' needs adequately, their shelves must always be stocked properly in all their outlets. This is a supply chain issue that can only be possible if they have a reliable network of truckers. Their solution? Well, they have so far hired more than 8,000 truckers directly to serve their business interests, with each trucker earning an average income of more than $80,000 annually. As a trucker, you play a big role in the success of so many companies.

Every year, trucking accounts for more than 70% of all the products transported within the US. That's more than 10 billion tons of cargo being hauled on our roads every year. Now, you may be tempted to think that, given these statistics, the market is already crowded and there may not be sufficient room for a new investor. Well, that's not true. If anything, there's still quite a shortage of truckers and investors in this industry. Industry experts believe that the trucking sector still needs roughly a million more truckers to meet the ever-growing demand. This means more room for growth, and investment opportunities for you.

In the year 2020, the trucking industry earned over $732 billion in gross revenue, which translates to around 80% of the national revenue from combined freight services, including air, water, and rail. This proves how important the trucking industry is to the entire economy.

The economic value of this business isn't limited to the revenues earned. Let's take the example of taxes. Taxation data from the past three years indicates that commercial trucks, on average, contribute more than $40 billion in taxes every year, yet they only comprise approximately 14% of the total number of registered vehicles on our roads.

Trucking is valuable even beyond our borders. For example, truckers delivered over 80% of the surface trade to Mexico and 70% to Canada in the year 2020 alone. It's important to note that this is also the year when most industries and countries worldwide were grounded because of Covid-19.

So far, the trucking industry employs more than 7.5 million people directly and indirectly in different capacities. According to a 2018 study by the Bureau of Labor Statistics, in the economy, 5.8% of the employed population accounts for 129 million full-time jobs.

When we talk of equal opportunity employers, no industry does this better than the trucking industry. Surprisingly, even as the national average rate of employment for minorities is just 22%, minorities make up more than 40% of the workforce in the trucking industry.

Based on this insight, we can consider the trucking industry a pillar of the economy. As our needs grow over time, so does the demand for more truckers to meet this surge in demand. Think about it for a moment—if all the truckers in the country were to go on strike, it would only take 2-3 days for most grocery stores in the country to run out of stock. A similar experience is possible in supermarkets all over the country. This further explains why some experts believe the trucking industry could use close to a million more truckers. This is true because it's not just the demands of the trucking industry that are growing, but the demands of the entire economy, and the first step is to accommodate what the industry needs by bringing more truckers into the business.

## How The Trucking Business Works

While investing in thriving industries like trucking is a brilliant idea, it's even wiser to understand the nitty-gritty of how that sector works. If you've been a player in the trucking industry before, this may be easier for you. However, if this is your first time, take your time and learn about the business first, then put your money forward. A good investment is one that you understand in and out.

The first thing you need to know about trucking is that it is a service industry. This means a business whose value is intangible. For example, while the trucks and goods transported in this sector are tangible, the service of trucking is not. Other examples of service industry businesses that you may know about include management, customer service, communications, banking, and software development.

Like every other business, you'll need to get certain licenses and permits to operate in this sector. For example, you'll need to get a Commercial Driver's License (CDL), which is the main foundation of driving commercial vehicles. There are three different classes of the CDL, Classes A, B, and C, each with varying requirements. If you are the primary trucker, you'll need the appropriate license. If you grow your business and decide to hire other truckers to work under your company, they must also have their licenses, since they'll be engaged in the actual business of trucking on a daily basis.

When applying for a license, note that other than the application fee, you'll also be charged an additional fee for each truck you own.

Other important permits that you must have to operate in this business include the International Fuel Tax Agreement (IFTA) license for which you will fill in the Blanket of Coverage (BOC-3) form, an International Registration Plan (IRP) tag, the Unified Carrier Registration (UCR), and you must also register your business with the Federal Motor Carrier Safety Administration (FMCSA), where you'll be issued with a motor carrier (MC) number.

Still within the FMCSA's mandate, you'll also be issued with a Federal (Department of Transportation) DOT number. Remember that this is one of the most heavily regulated industries in the country, so it's more than just finding a truck and a trucking route. As the backbone of the economy, you must adhere to set regulations and standards all the time. The DOT number we mentioned is used to track your compliance with the industry regulations and your company's safety records on the road.

Trucking isn't just about getting into the truck and delivering goods from one place to the next. Like every other business, there are other operations behind the scenes that support the primary aspect of trucking. These are the back-office operations that are equally important to your success in this industry.

While your trucks will move products, back-office operations are the engine that keeps your entire business running. For example, this is where you coordinate all the dispatch in real-time, especially when you start hiring new drivers. You must also have an efficient communication platform to interact with all your team members. Other important back-office operations include insurance, researching the market and setting prices, handling all the paperwork, marketing, and advertising.

From time to time, you'll move high-value goods or goods of an extremely sensitive nature, like weapons. Such are the times when your integrity and business ethics will be tested. In such cases, other crucial issues arise, like the kind of risks you take, and the legal aspects that comes with it. Granted, given the nature of some goods, the safety of your trucks, drivers, and the cargo being ferried will always be a concern until they arrive at their destination. This is true even for normal goods that we wouldn't necessarily classify as high-value or sensitive cargo.

To make a name for yourself in this industry, you must be energetic, up-to-date with the industry rules and regulations, and most importantly, remember that your business integrity will go a long way in creating and establishing a good reputation for your business.

## What's Bad for Business

As much as it is important to understand the finer details of the business, it's equally important to know the unhealthy business practices that may derail your trucking operation. Businesses fail from time to time, and not necessarily because they were unable to turn a profit or because the conditions in the business environment were unfavorable. Many businesses fail because of lack of appropriate internal structures to support the operation. Let's discuss five crucial, yet common issues in the trucking sector that are bad for business, so you know what to avoid when you set up your operation.

### 1. Unclear Leadership

As the business owner, you must be clear on your vision, goals, objectives, and strategies for the business. This is even more important when you have an entire team working for you. Without clear guidelines, you end up with a chaotic business model where no one knows what they are supposed to do, or who to approach for different things. When everyone is clear on their purpose and role in your business, it's easier to streamline the entire business process in a manner that sets your business up for success.

## 2. Flawed Growth Strategy

A good growth strategy is necessary to ensure that you are growing the business in the right direction. This also means focusing on more than what's going on in the market today. It means planning for the business years into the future. It works hand in hand with a clear leadership structure to ensure that everyone is focused on working and thinking long-term.

If your current growth strategy isn't suited for long-term growth, it is flawed from the start and will hinder your business growth. Think of the strategy as an elaborate roadmap or plan that helps you analyze your performance today, and how you can use it for future growth.

## 3. Lousy Work Culture

To succeed in the trucking business, and any other business really, you must create a healthy work environment. Unfortunately, this isn't always the case. Many businesses fail because of lousy, or toxic, work cultures. These are business environments where selfishness, mistrust, gossip, clique culture, and hostility are the norm. As you can imagine, it's hard to succeed in such environments because people are working against one another. In such an environment, people feel emotionally and psychologically drained, which affects their loyalty.

## 4. Poor Economics

You must always stay on top of the company economics. How are your cash flows? If you have more money moving out of the business than coming in, you are in big trouble. One of the first signs that your business is struggling and might actually fail, is a negative cash flow position. However, you must also understand that businesses go through cycles when you incur more expenses than income. This, for a few weeks or months, is normal, especially if it is a common experience throughout the industry. However, if your negative cash flows persist when the trend has reversed in the entire industry, there's a good chance you are heading for trouble.

As a first-time trucking business, you may also struggle during the initial months to get on your feet, which is also normal. However, if this persists, it may be a warning sign that you need to rethink your investment.

## 5. Inability to Handle the Competition

Competition is both normal and healthy in business. The trucking sector, like every other industry, thrives because of competition. Competition challenges businesses to innovate and get creative. It makes you think outside the box to find ways of creating more value for your business. It is the incentive that makes some businesses succeed where others fail.

If you are unable to handle the competition, there's a good chance your business will fail. This isn't just about your inability to compete, but it points to your inability to innovate, get creative or come up with better business strategies to outdo your competitors.

There are many other issues that are not healthy for your operation, which you will learn from experience as you run the business. However, the most important thing is that you need to be receptive to new ideas, and always stay informed and updated about changes in the trucking sector.

## Investment Success Formula

There are six crucial forces that affect your possibility of success. We will break these down into two groups: wealth builders and wealth killers. As you can already tell, these forces will either help you generate wealth, or limit your ability to do so.

### *Wealth Builders*

### 1. Amount

The concept of building wealth is to keep growing what you already have. Therefore, assuming that all other factors remain unchanged, you have better opportunities when you have more to save and invest, which loosely translates to more wealth. Your only challenge is to create a saving habit, because many people actually struggle to save.

### 2. Time

It's often advisable to start investing at an early age, even if it's just a little amount of money. The secret here is to take advantage of the power of compounding, as used in compound interest. The longer you invest, the higher chances you have of greater returns.

## 3. Rate

The rate of return, together with the time and amount of investment money you have, is the final piece of the jigsaw to building wealth. A higher rate generally means higher returns. However, you must also understand that in most cases, high returns usually mean you take more risks than usual.

## *Wealth Killers*

## 1. Fees

Fees are normal in any investment. However, the problem comes in when some fees are hidden in the fine print, so without realizing it, you end up losing much of your investment returns to hidden fees, hurting your wealth-building efforts.

## 2. Tax

Taxes, like fees, are also expected, not just in investments, but in most financial transactions in life. When the taxes applicable are too complicated, they undermine your success at wealth building. However, you can still take additional measures to reduce their impact, like using tax-free savings accounts.

## 3. Inflation

Inflation is always a thorn in the flesh, not just for investors, but for everyone else. This is true because of the fact that it erodes your purchasing power over time. Rising inflation means that it will cost you considerably more to buy the same amount of goods and services you could afford earlier. Since you can't control inflation, you must look for smart ways of working around it.

The six points we've mentioned before are crucial in understanding how your money works. It's important to learn not just how to make more money, but also some of the potential challenges that may derail your financial plans, and come up with smart ways of working around them.

## Checklist and CDL Minded Approach

Our discussion so far has prepared you for the finer details, and you should be getting practical information and tips on trucking and how the industry works. This will help you figure out whether the business is profitable for you or not, and more importantly, to prepare you mentally and financially to get into trucking. You can understand the profitability of the business and how the CDL Industry works by using the following checklist:

| Activity | What to look for | Complete? Yes or No |
|---|---|---|
| Research the industry | Learn vital information about the trucking industry. You're looking for information like how much drivers earn, the working conditions, challenges they face, and so on. | |

| | | |
|---|---|---|
| Interview owner-operators | This should give you a better view of the business from owner-operators. Consult a few owner-operators and learn about their experience, the challenges they face, the important lessons, their regrets, and any words of advice they can give a beginner like yourself. | |
| Permits and licenses | As you speak to different people in the industry, also find out more about the licenses and permits, the CDL classes, the costs, any new licensing changes you should know about. | |
| Avoiding failure | As you interact with truck drivers, find out their opinion on why some trucking companies have collapsed, and what they felt could have been done differently. | |
| Assess competition | Interview drivers to find out the impact of competition on their business. On what grounds do they compete? How do they handle an aggressive competitor? What good or bad results have come from stiff competition? | |

# CHAPTER 4

# MAKING BIG BUCKS FROM TRUCKS

From the lessons you have learned so far about risk and choosing the right investments, you are now in a better position to learn different strategies you can use to make money in the trucking business. Trucking remains the backbone of the economy, especially when we consider its role in building a modern society. It's through trucking that every sector of the economy thrives. From delivering raw materials to production centers to getting finished products to retail outlets, trucking makes it all possible.

As your interest in this industry peaks, it's important to understand how trucking companies make money. This will help you figure out whether you are ready to invest in this industry, and if so, how to go about it.

## How Do Truck Companies Make Money?

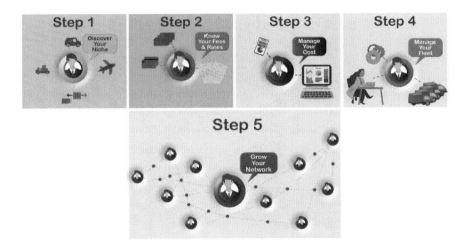

We've described them as the backbone of the economy so far, as they move goods from one place to the other. In our introductory chapter, we further mentioned that there's a massive shortage of truck drivers in this business, which means more growth opportunities for new and existing drivers. To tap into this potential, it's wise to understand the different ways to make money in this industry by first understanding the five simple steps to working, growing and transforming your business.

- **Step 1: Discover Your Niche**

# Step 1

The first thing you'll learn about the trucking business is that it's not a one-size-fits-all market. There are different niches in the trucking and transportation business due to the fact that customers have varying needs. For example, customers who deal in fresh seafood have different needs from those who deal in household furniture, yet they all need truckers.

As you get into the business, therefore, you must first figure out your desired niche. Study the needs of customers in that particular segment, and come up with innovative ways of addressing them. Do that, and you'll be on your way to trucking wealth.

- ***Step 2: Fees and Rates (Know Your Fees and Rates)***

The amount you charge for trucking services will either earn you or cost you customers, which means it directly affects the success or failure of your business. Many new truckers struggle with setting the right prices for their services. Research the market to understand the market rates, then from there, perform an elaborate cost-benefit analysis to establish the right competitive prices.

Remember that while you are free to set your prices, you must also think of your competitors and your operating costs. At the end of the day, you are here to run a profit-making business, so your rates must also be sensible. The goal is to strike a healthy balance between making profits and giving customers a good deal.

- ### *Step 3: Cost Management (Manage Your Cost)*

# Step 3

One of the common beginner mistakes we discussed in Chapter 2 was letting costs and losses get out of hand. The success of your business is directly proportional to your ability to manage costs, not just in trucking, but in every other sector of our economy. In other words, the growth of your business ties directly into managing your costs from all aspects of the business. There are several cost centers in the trucking business, some of which you may not have the power to influence.

Look at things like management and clerical costs, accounting, the cost of fuel, wear and tear, maintenance, and getting the right personnel to work for you. Even though you may not be able to influence or control some of these costs, you must be aware of them, and take measures to limit your exposure where possible. Efficient cost management can help you avoid running into unnecessary losses.

- *Step 4: Fleet Management (Manage Your Fleet)*

# Step 4

While there's a lot of management and administrative work that goes into running an efficient trucking operation, the core of your business involves trucks and commercial vehicles. Therefore, you must ensure your trucks are efficiently managed. Anything that affects the performance and reliability of your trucks will affect your profit margins.

For example, if your trucks are not properly serviced, they'll not be fuel-efficient and might be prone to frequent breakdowns. If this describes your operation, you won't be able to measure up to the competition. If anything, in an industry with lots of opportunities, you'll struggle to get those opportunities. Remember that inefficiency on your trucks means that you won't meet customer deadlines, so you'll soon lose customers too.

### ▪ *Step 5: The Power of Networking (Grow Your Network)*

# Step 5

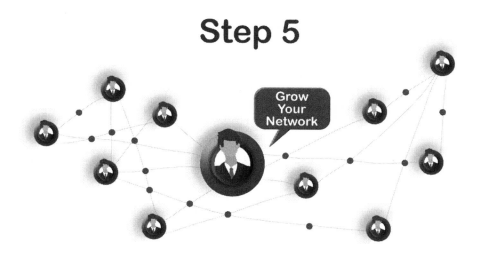

Trucking is one of those businesses where your net worth is greatly influenced by your network. Sure, you may get a few business deals here and there if you decide to go it alone, but that won't be sustainable over the long term. To build a successful and thriving trucking operation, you need a healthy network of clients, owner-operators and truckers.

Without a healthy network, you'll be relying on a few sources to get your business, which is not sustainable either. Networks get you repeat business and referrals, and this is also how you grow your business name over time while earning more profit in the trucking and transportation business.

## Assessing Profitability in the Trucking Industry

For a fact, trucking is unlike other businesses. Generally, when more players come into the market, profit margins get thinner. In the trucking industry, however, the fact that there's still a shortage of truckers means that there are more than enough opportunities for everyone, and then some.

Is the business profitable? Yes, it is.

Not even the 2020 Covid pandemic could stop the trucking industry. Like other sectors, the trucking industry experienced some shocks, but it bounced back, even stronger, and we can anticipate more growth in the foreseeable future.

Unfortunately, new truckers still struggle in this industry. By emphasizing the points we discussed in the previous section, you'll put yourself above the rest, and start operating your trucking business with the confidence of someone who has been in the industry for decades.

To run and maintain a profitable trucking business, you must be a careful planner. Plan for everything, from managing your finances to hiring the right business partners, to move your business forward. Learn from experienced truckers how to cut costs without affecting your efficiency, and more importantly, learn how to manage your cash flows.

It's not just about building a profitable CDL trucking and transportation business; it's also about keeping the business profitable for the long term. So, how do you stay profitable in the CDL trucking business? Let's go over some simple approaches that you can implement right away:

## Service Pricing

Building on our earlier point on fees and rates, pricing is an important determinant in the profitability of your venture. You set prices after factoring in expenses like arrangements with brokers, compensating your drivers, fuel allocation, and the cost of using software in your operation. Once you have these figured out, you can then come up with a competitive pricing strategy that will earn you profits.

For competitive price ranges, find a trucking lane. A trucking lane is a route that a specific carrier uses frequently, also known as a shipping lane or a freight lane. Consistency is what helps you understand applicable prices. Consult a few brokers or load boards to understand the average shipping prices for every directional haul. With this information, you can then add your business markup of up to 15%. That is how you establish an ideal service pricing range.

## Cash Flow Planning

Beyond service pricing, the next important step to staying profitable in this business is to make sure your cash flow position is healthy, positive and secure. If anything, this is crucial to your operation because cash flow management is an everyday affair. You don't want to be releasing more cash than you have to. Naturally, broker and shipper payments are generally delayed by 15–45 days. With this in mind, you need a financing approach to ensure your operations don't stall because of pending payments.

A simple approach is to speak to your preferred lender about establishing a line of credit, usually with your unpaid invoices as security for the financing. Some lenders may also accept your operational equipment as collateral, a program known as equipment financing. Even as you consider these options, which have helped many small truckers grow their businesses, make sure you are getting favorable rates from lenders. Research well in order to find lending terms that will not cripple or limit your growth.

## *Make More Money*

Now, an important lesson about any business is that making more money generally solves most of your profitability problems. Take a moment and think about the evolution and resilience of the trucking industry. Over the years, this industry has stood the test of time. From environmental regulations to global pandemics, economic crises, and revolutionary technology, trucking still stands tall.

Since the structure of the industry makes it defy all the odds, there are two simple actions you can take to defy the odds on your end, and run a profitable trucking business:

First, you need to understand your unit costs. It's impossible to come up with a realistic and profitable price range for your services unless you know how much it costs you to run the business, on a mile-by-mile basis. This is what we call unit costs. In short, how much are you making for every mile of cargo hauled?

A true estimate must include both your fixed and variable costs, or business overhead and running costs respectively. Record all your expenses, including office supplies and everything else, while your truck is on the road. Even those expenses that seem insignificant are valuable when you look at the bigger picture.

Keep neat and accurate daily, weekly, and monthly records, which make it easier to analyze your transactions over time. This is where a good bookkeeper comes in handy. With clear, accurate data, it will be easier to establish your unit costs for every mile covered. This may also be useful for tax purposes.

Second, you need to pick up more loaded miles. Loaded miles refers to the duration when your trucks are in use, loaded with customer property. This is important because it means you are getting paid for those miles.

Now, we must also mention that loaded miles do not include empty miles, also known as deadhead miles. Empty miles refer to the time duration when your trucks are empty while being on the road; perhaps they are in between loads, traveling to collect a load, or returning to your base of operation after completing a delivery.

Ideally, loaded miles are the reason why you are in business. You get paid when your trucks are carrying customers' property (or if you are transporting passengers, getting paid by the hour or a fixed cost per trip is how you get paid). Therefore, try to get as many loaded miles as you can. If your truck delivers property somewhere, try and make sure it doesn't make the return trip empty. Remember that you are fighting with other startups and established companies with fleets for the same loads. With this in mind, you must be relentless in the business. Use every approach at your disposal to get loads into your trucks. This is also where networking will come in handy.

## How to Make Passive Income From Trucking

From everything we've discussed in this chapter, you now have a good idea about how money moves in the trucking industry, and how to set competitive, profitable prices. Next, we look at practical options where you can apply these lessons and start earning right away. Note that these are also great opportunities to build passive cash flows from the trucking business. We mentioned earlier that the trucking industry is filled with opportunities, so let's discuss some of them now:

- Leasing Trucks

This is a common option for many beginners, particularly if you don't have your own trucks. You can lease a semi-truck for business use. Naturally, the owner (lessor) will assess your viability, especially your creditworthiness, to see if you are credible to lease the vehicle. You are simply renting the truck, so it's a good option for someone who doesn't have enough to buy a truck. You can also get into a lease-to-buy agreement if you wish to buy the truck in the future.

- FedEx Delivery Routes

Deliveries are the in-thing in our society at the moment. You can make money delivering everything from food to groceries to furniture. Prompt deliveries are the icing on the cake for a thriving online shopping culture, and this is where you come in. With a truck, you can deliver more than the average delivery guy on his bike or car, which means that with the right planning, you can earn more per hour on deliveries since you don't have size limitations. You can have furniture in the back of your truck, and birthday cakes in front.

Building on this, you can also buy a FedEx route. This simply means you become the go-to delivery person for FedEx deliveries in a specific territory and get paid for every delivery. Now, an interesting thing about FedEx routes is that they generally assign you their own trucks, so you may not even need to have your own.

FedEx allows you two alternatives for this service. You can either buy the ground pickup and delivery route, or a linehaul route. Linehaul routes are longer, so you'll need a semi-truck for that. Ground pickup and delivery routes are local deliveries which can be accomplished with box trucks or vans.

The beauty of working with FedEx is that you are guaranteed deliveries every other day, especially for ground pickup and delivery routes. This takes away the hassle of looking for loads. All you have to do is deliver on time. The fact that you can use box trucks and vans also makes this a viable option for a first-timer, especially if you can't afford a semi-truck yet.

- Bread Routes

This is similar to the FedEx approach, only you'll be delivering bread instead, within a specific territory. The concept here is to earn on each loaf of bread sold to retailers and supermarkets within your assigned territory. Bread routes are a reliable source of income since most of the big-name distributors prefer exclusivity in their delivery arrangements. Therefore, if you sign up with a retailer like Target or Walmart, they'll only buy bread through you. What's even better about this arrangement is that you'll start earning from day one.

- Landscaping Services

A pickup will be more than sufficient for this. Other than your pickup, you'll also need to get equipment like a shovel, rake and a lawnmower. Register your company and start advertising in your neighborhood and beyond, depending on your intended business strategy.

- Dump Truck Services

If you're excited about the aspect of long hauls, short hauls, and junk removal services such as hauling dirt, asphalt, and other contaminated materials, the dump trucking industry may be a suitable opportunity for you. You can offer this service locally or expand to other neighborhoods. Besides, the fact that your drivers get to come home to their families every evening is a bonus. This service may also complement landscaping, so think of how you can do both.

- Equipment Leasing

Crowdsourcing is so common today, and you can also use that concept to make money in the trucking business. There are many crowdsourcing apps where you can rent your trucks to customers for different purposes. Some examples include Bungii, Dolly, Turo, GoShare, Buddytruk, Bellhop, and Lugg. Instead of having the truck lying idle in your garage, you can lease it out in your local area and beyond, and earn some money.

- Snow Plowing

Most trucks are built for durability, stability, and versatility. Therefore, it's no surprise that snow plowing features on this list. During the winter, you can put your truck to use and clear driveways and other areas for customers, especially if your region receives a lot of snow.

- Truck Advertisement

You can also talk to product managers about using your truck as an advertisement platform to promote their brand. Discuss the dynamics with them, put their ads on your truck and go on with your business as usual. You can earn a decent amount every week or month through this advertisement approach.

- Construction

The construction industry and trucks are a match made in heaven. There are different types of jobs in the construction industry that are suitable for your truck. From deliveries to hauling equipment, there's always something your truck can do at a construction site.

- Hauling Services

If there's one thing that trucks are built for, it has to be hauling. From heavy to wide loads, most trucks will do the job. While some cars can do the same task, trucks do it better. Therefore, some people prefer to hire trucks for their hauling needs instead of risking damage to their cars. This is probably one of the easiest ways to get paid passively with your truck. In the same vein, you can also discuss a business arrangement with a mattress return service in your area. The concept is as simple as getting paid to deliver a mattress.

You can also outsource your work to a professional by hiring a driver and a manager or VA (virtual assistant) to run, manage and operate your business so you can effortlessly enjoy your company without being a slave to it.

As you can clearly see, owning a truck comes with a lot of income-earning opportunities. These are great opportunities to make money while you continue working on something else, or as most people say, while you sleep. It's as simple as setting up your trucking business the right way and letting your money work for you.

Weigh your options, consider the risks, costs, and any other factors involved, and then let your truck bring in some money for you and your family. Trucking is a thriving industry, and all you have to do is figure out how you can profit from it. The best thing about it is that you can either become an active, passive or residual investor, so the choice is yours.

## Checklist and CDL Minded Approach

Throughout this chapter, we've attempted to answer the question "How can I make money from trucking?" We discussed a lot of useful ideas, but let's face it, unless you are setting up several trucking and transportation businesses, you can't really invest in each and every one of those ideas. The secret is to try and find a niche that interests you, and then from there, learn how to work around it.

Use the following checklist to learn how to earn passive income from trucking while you're asleep.

| Activity | What to look for | Complete? Yes or No |
|---|---|---|
| Route management | Interview drivers on how they manage their routes, which routes are profitable, and anything else that may be useful. | |
| Managing costs | Learn about the different types of costs you will incur when running a trucking business. Start with the fixed costs, then the recurring variable costs, and common miscellaneous costs that are not so easy to classify as fixed or variable. | |
| Networking | Networking goes a long way in this industry. Find out about networking opportunities or events where you can meet and interact with drivers and other stakeholders. | |
| Avoiding empty miles | Talk to drivers and owner-operators about the strategies they use to make sure they never travel empty. | |
| Setting prices | Trucking is a highly competitive industry, so research and learn how to set prices that keep you profitable while still meeting your customers' needs. | |
| Passive income | We discussed many opportunities for earning passive income. Review those that might interest you and research the market to see if they are viable. You can also talk to other drivers and owner-operators to find out what else they do on the side. | |

# CHAPTER 5

# GETTING THE RIGHT EQUIPMENT IN PLACE

S uccess in trucking involves having the right tools, equipment, and an innovative business mindset. Without the right tools and equipment, there's not much you can do with the right mindset. You can think of brilliant ideas, but it's the tools and equipment that make your ideas practical.

You generally have two options—either to buy or rent equipment for your business. As you can imagine, the ideal option comes down to how much money you have, and how much you are willing to commit to sourcing equipment.

There are different types of equipment you can use in this business. The challenge for most people is usually finding the right one. Remember, just because something is good, doesn't mean it's suitable for you. The secret is to match your trucking and transportation business needs with the right equipment. Here are three useful tips to guide you:

## 1. The Nature of Your Business

You have to decide the kind of operation you intend to run. Is your trucking business interstate or intrastate? Interstate simply means driving from one state to another, while intrastate means local work within your state.

This decision will greatly influence every aspect of your equipment purchase. For example, if your business is mostly interstate, your truck should be comfortable enough to live in and drive on the open road, since the interstate requires you to travel long distances (either across state lines, across the region or even throughout the country).

If we are going with the interstate option, you must also consider fuel consumption. Your options should be specific to trucks that are highly rated on fuel economy. Why is this important? It's simple, really—from time to time, you'll be hauling cargo on roads with very few gas stations, or a great distance from one to the next. The last thing you want is to be stranded in the middle of nowhere with customer cargo and no fuel. This is actually a security risk.

For intrastate trucking, the opposite of these scenarios is mostly true. However, you must still make decisions that align with your overall business objectives.

## 2. New Versus Used Equipment

This decision is mostly about your personal preferences, amount of capital and the nature of your business. With new equipment, it may be a while before you need to worry about repairs or replacing parts. Note, however, that this peace of mind comes at a steep cost. Most reliable new trucks cost upwards of $70,000.

Alternatively, you can get a used truck for a fraction of that price. Used trucks will still get the job done, especially if the previous owner was diligent and strict on usage, care and maintenance. For an intrastate business, for example, it may not make financial sense to buy a new truck. Should you opt for a used truck, ensure it's not too old to serve your needs. Apart from that, inspect for wear and tear, and the mileage covered. With some research and a good mechanic, you can find a good used truck that will serve you well without bleeding your young business dry.

## 3. Buy Versus Leasing

Generally, buying a truck can be intimidating for new truckers, especially when we consider the price of the truck. However, when you buy a truck, especially a new one, most dealers allow you the benefit of trading it in for a new model in the future. Some even allow you to use the truck as a down payment for another.

But buying a truck isn't always a realistic option for everyone. Owner-operators, especially those who have more than ten years of experience in the business, seem to prefer leasing. Lenders are more willing to negotiate favorable leasing arrangements with them because of their experience. That being said, the fundamental rule of leasing is that you must have good credit.

From the three points we've discussed before, you can now take the next step to find the right equipment for your business. Let's briefly mention some factors that will guide you on this path, and their importance in your decision-making:

- An elaborate investment plan

Before you buy any equipment, always assess its pros and cons against your business needs to determine the potential return on investment (ROI). For example, even though buying new equipment may be an attractive proposition, it may make more financial sense for you to buy used equipment. Remember that you still have other aspects of the business to run, and they all need money.

- Equipment viability

This is purely about being realistic. What is it about the equipment you want to buy that will increase your chances of success in the business? Does it give you an edge above your competitors? These kinds of questions can help you avoid falling prey to aggressive marketing schemes that don't add immediate value to your business.

- Consult an expert

It always helps to talk to an expert before buying any trucking equipment. They'll help you understand whether the equipment will match your business needs, in terms of resource utilization or handling your business capacity comfortably. The simplest approach here is usually a cost-benefit analysis to determine whether the equipment is worth buying.

- Innovate

Don't just buy equipment for your business, buy equipment that can fit into your innovative plans to beat the competition. In this business, innovation consists of improved efficiency and better service delivery, while keeping your running costs as reasonably low as possible. The right equipment helps you streamline your business processes, improve your services, and break into profitable niche markets.

- Think long-term

Even though you are buying equipment to meet an immediate need, the purchase must still align with your long-term business objectives. If you are not planning long-term, your purchases may be useful right now, but prove too costly in the future. This is also why it's advisable to speak to an expert in the trucking industry to help you understand the dynamics of not just your business, but the trucking and transportation industry in general, with respect to equipment purchases.

- Explore your options

One of the best things about buying anything today is the power of the internet. You have so much variety to choose from. Don't jump at the first equipment you come across. Take your time and research everything from internet listings, trade fairs, auctions, and newspaper listings before you buy equipment.

- The cost of training

As you search for the right equipment, remember to factor in the cost of training. If the equipment is too complex for your team, their productivity may drop for a while as they get acquainted with the new processes. With that being said, complex or not, you must always plan for a brief period of disruption as your team learns how to handle the equipment.

- Financing the purchase

Whether you are paying for the equipment in cash or through lender financing, you must consider the pros and cons of the financing options available to you. Even though each financier has different financing terms, your business experience and credit rating will always give you better bargaining power. Discuss financing terms with different lenders, then compare their offers and choose one that caters to your needs accordingly.

## Consider Your Options

If there's one thing you'll really appreciate about trucking, it's the fact that there's so much diversity in the kind of equipment you can use in your business. Let's walk you through different types of trucks you may come across:

## 1. Cube truck

This is also known as a box truck, box van, cube van, or straight truck. They are famously used for transporting small items, home goods, and furniture and can carry a maximum cargo load of up to 10,000 pounds.

## 2. Conestoga trailers

This is a special truck built for versatility and designed to protect your freight from the weather elements, thanks to the retractable tarp system that covers the entire deck. They can load up to 45,000 pounds of cargo.

## 3. Enclosed trailer

Also known as a dry van trailer, this truck is also designed to protect your cargo from the harsh weather elements. Some enclosed trailers come with liftgates which make it easier to load cargo on and off the truck. They can also load up to 45,000 pounds of cargo.

## 4. Flatbed trailers

These trucks have neither a roof nor side, and are commonly used to transport wide, oversized or heavy cargo. The ease of loading cargo onto flatbeds makes them an industry favorite because of their versatility, and they can haul up to 48,000 pounds of cargo.

## 5. Double drop trailers

These are also known as lowboy, low loaders, float, or low-bed trailers. It is a semi-trailer that comes with a drop deck, hence the name double drop trailers in some instances. They are commonly used to haul cargo whose height cannot be handled by flatbed trailers. They can carry up to 40,000 pounds of cargo, though with more axles, they can carry double the weight.

## 6. Reefer trailers

These are also known as refrigerated trailers. They are specially designed trailers with temperature control units, specifically designed to transport frozen, chilled, or any other fresh item that may require refrigeration while in transit. The temperature control feature means that the cargo will be maintained at a specific temperature, regardless of the temperature outside the truck. Note that refrigeration means that you'll spend more on fuel to keep the cooling system running. They mostly haul up to 45,000 pounds of cargo.

## 7. Removable gooseneck (RGN) trailers

RGNs are some of the most versatile trucks in the business, especially since they are built to load large cargo that generally wouldn't fit into most enclosed trucks. You can actually detach the front and lower the truck to the ground, allowing you to drive cargo-like vehicles right onto the RGN trailer. Most of these trucks are used to ferry large, tall, or long cargo. By default, RGNs can haul up to 45,000 pounds. However, with up to 20 additional axles, this limit increases to 150,000 pounds.

## 8. Specialized trailers

As the name suggests, these trucks are uniquely built for special cargo. These trucks generally don't fit the normal descriptions we assign to other kinds of trucks, as they are built for specific purposes. Examples include oil trailers, logging trailers, car carriers, and cattle haulers. They are uniquely designed to suit the intended purpose.

## 9. Step deck trailers

Also known as single-drop or drop deck trailers, these trucks are a modification of the traditional flatbed, though they are built to haul cargo that the normal flatbed wouldn't be able to. They have no doors, roof, or sides, and simply look like a moving platform. They can haul up to 48,000 pounds of cargo.

## 10. Stretch trailers

These trailers can be extended lengthwise and are built to haul cargo whose length cannot fit the standard RGN truck. When hauling cargo using stretch trailers, the overall weight of the truck determines the number of axles needed. The average stretch trailer can haul up to 45,000 pounds, but considerably higher with more axles attached.

## 11. Dump truck

These trucks are used to transport loose materials in large volumes, for example, demolition waste, gravel, sand, garbage, and dirt. Most large dump trucks can haul up to 28,000 pounds, while smaller dump trucks handle up to 15,000 pounds.

## 12. Other CDL transportation vehicles

Other types of commercial vehicles include transit buses, (also known as accordion or articulated buses), coach buses and school buses. While we've mostly talked about transporting cargo, the CDL transportation industry also involves transporting passengers.

Transit buses are high-capacity buses that are used for high-capacity passenger transport. Their high capacity makes them ideal for bus rapid transport (BRT) and transportation systems that allow for faster boarding and disembarking because of their larger doors than the average bus. Not only are they more stable due to the lower center of gravity, and have better fuel economy than most normal buses, but they are always in demand for drivers and transportation for passengers as well.

Coach buses simply transport people from one place to another. You can get a contract with a company to transport their staff from their homes or a central point to work and back in the evening. Some can include day trips and overnight trips as well.

The same applies to school buses, where your arrangement will be to pick up kids from a certain neighborhood and drop them off at school, and do the reverse in the evening. There are also school field trips and after school activities as well.

## Tips for Buying the Right Equipment

At this point, you understand the value of getting the right equipment for your business. So, how do you go about it? What must you do to match your equipment needs and equipment choices in the market?

The best choice comes down to your priorities. What are you looking for in the truck? What do you want to get from it? How will it assist your business? How long do you plan on using the truck?

In this business, your emphasis should be on longevity and reliability. There are several reputable brands in the market that stand out on these metrics, so that would be a brilliant place to start a conversation with your salesman.

At this point, you should have already made up your mind on whether you are getting a used truck or a new one. Here are four important factors that will help you buy the right equipment:

### *The Salesperson*

Most people think of salespeople as only out to meet their sales targets and earn commissions. This isn't always true. If anything, a good salesperson can be a useful asset when buying trucking equipment. Look for someone that not only has a good reputation in the industry but also has years of experience in selling trucks. Given the nature of this industry, that will almost certainly be a referral.

Once you find the salesperson, talk to them about the type of truck you are looking for. We mentioned different types of trucks a while back, so you have an idea of the kind of options you are working with. Ultimately, your choice comes down to the kind of work your truck will be doing.

## The Dealership

Repair and maintenance are a normal and necessary part of the trucking business. You need a dealership or repair shop that's as close to you as possible, considering the kind of work that your trucks will be doing. This is purely about convenience, but will also save you a great deal of time, energy, and money.

A dealership closer to you means that there's a high chance you can create a good personal relationship with their team. You may even have them pick up your truck at home and deliver it once the repairs are done, as you handle other items on your to-do list for the day. That's the power of your network building your net worth.

## The Mechanic

The most important things you need in a mechanic are reliability and competence. The easiest way around this is to consult other truck drivers for referrals, especially those who've been in the business for years. Note, however, that even the most competent mechanic may not be reliable all the time. For example, they would be of no use to you if you must book them three or four months in advance. To be safe, find two or three mechanics you can rely on, because there's no guarantee that their schedule will always be open for you on demand.

## The Best Deal

You may get incredible deals when you buy from a trucking company. Large companies trade in their trucks from time to time, or retire them in line with their company policy. Some of their commercial vehicles may be decent enough for your business model. Besides, since most large companies have exclusive contracts with some of the best mechanics and dealerships in the country, you can easily review their repair and maintenance history to get a better understanding of the truck's performance record.

## Tips for Buying Used Equipment

Let's face it, buying used trucks, or any other equipment for that matter, can be a huge gamble. However, people get amazing deals on used equipment all the time. How do they do it? What's their secret? Well, there really is no secret. It's as simple as conducting your due diligence, and everything else will be okay. Here are some useful tips to help you navigate the tricky market for used equipment:

- Always request the maintenance record for the truck. This will give you a good idea of the engine health, and whether the truck will actually meet your business needs in its present condition.

- Know what you are getting into. With the right care and maintenance, most decent engines can power your business for up to a million miles. However, you must also factor in the cost of repairs and replacing parts, and most importantly, how soon you'll need to do that. Does the cost still sound reasonable?

- Relationships are of utmost importance in this market. Unless you have a personal relationship with the seller, it's always wise to buy from reputable dealers who have years of experience dealing with used trucks.

- If the dealership offers an extended warranty, find out the limit of their coverage. More often, extended warranties are quite expensive, and don't necessarily cover all the part repairs and replacements for your truck.

- Be careful while shopping for used trucks, since some of them may already be on their deathbed, collecting dust in the grave-yard site of non-working trucks. If the price looks too good to be true, it most likely is, so find out more about that truck model and parts. If that particular truck is available in the market at a low price, you should probably avoid it.

- Know when to walk away from a deal. Visible signs of an accident, and no maintenance history, are some reasons why you should walk away. Some dealerships buy problematic trucks cheaply, perform some cosmetic work on them, and flip them for a decent profit.

- Consider buying a used truck from fleets. Companies that own fleets generally have a replacement plan, so they periodically change their old trucks for newer models. You can get more than just the proof of regular maintenance and mechanical history. Some dealers may even connect you with the previous driver to give you a better perspective of their experience on the truck. You must know, however, that some drivers are quite rough on company trucks, since they don't personally incur any costs.

Finally, you must never let your guard down when buying a used truck. No detail is ever too small to be insignificant. Research well and ask all the questions you need to. At the end of the day, you'll be the one who ends up with a good used truck, or a bad used truck, depending on your mindset and strategy.

## Checklist and CDL Minded Approach

| Activity | What to look for | Complete? Yes or no. If yes, what did you do to complete this task? If not, what stopped you from achieving it? |
|---|---|---|
| Your business model | The idea here is to figure out the right truck for your business idea. We discussed different types of trucks to help you with this decision, so review and make a choice. | |
| Truck type | Decide whether you are buying a new truck or a used truck. | |
| Ownership | Consider your options between buying and leasing the truck. | |

| | | |
|---|---|---|
| Financing | Visit different lenders to discuss financing, whether you qualify, and other options they can provide beyond purchasing the truck, like supporting your business through invoice processing. Here you are also trying to establish a good working relationship with your lenders. | |
| Window shopping | Since you are now aware of your financing position, it's time to find a truck. Visit dealerships, talk to the salespeople and mechanics. Learn about the trucks that fit your budget. | |
| The garage | You will need a garage for your trucks. Visit a few garages and talk to them about the type of truck you intend to buy. Learn about its common issues, maintenance guide, fuel consumption, and anything else you should know about. | |
| Business management systems | Research and talk to people in the industry about the kind of systems they use for back-office operations. This will include things like document processors, accounting programs, fleet management applications, and so on. | |

# CHAPTER 6

# TRUCKING TECHNOLOGIES YOU MUST KNOW

Technology exists to help us refine processes and make life better. Every sector of our economy relies on technology in one way or the other. Even something as simple as accessing this book is all about technology. As you venture into the trucking and transportation business, it is vital that you learn some of the key trucking technologies that can help you make smart decisions and drive your business towards prosperity.

If there's one thing we've learned about technology, it's that it keeps changing over time because what works today may not necessarily work tomorrow, therefore you must keep adapting to the changes.

## Impact of Technologies on Investments

Before we get into the different types of technologies available in the trucking and transportation business, we should first understand how technology has revolutionized the investment business. Thanks to the cutting-edge technologies, investment is no longer limited to wealthy or older people who have years of experience. You can approach any investment opportunity confidently, research, scale the markets and earn decent profits. Let's briefly mention some of the crucial ways technology has impacted investment, that will be useful to you in the transportation and trucking business:

### *Effective Communication*

Things change in the investment markets so frequently that it's a must to have consistent, clear, and reliable communication, especially if you invest with a financial advisor. You must be able to get in touch with them as soon as possible so that you don't miss out on great opportunities.

It's not just about the opportunities available in the market; it's also about what you can do to protect your business portfolio. Before investing with any broker or financial advisor, always find out their preferred communication channels and their availability. Timely and reliable communication with your financial advisor can help you prevent losses and make investment decisions that enhance the overall value of your portfolio.

## Improved Financial Planning

Let's face it, you've interacted with different financial planning programs, apps or websites before. Your interaction may have been influenced by personal or business reasons. However, one thing that cuts across most of these programs is the desire to understand your financial situation. Once you understand your financial standing, it's easier to make investment decisions that don't put your entire financial portfolio at risk. You have access to all kinds of financial tools for different purposes, from market volatility to budgeting tools.

## Investment Security

As we embrace the benefits of technology, it's only fair that we also become aware of the drawbacks. Granted, many people make financial transactions online today. It's simpler, faster, and more convenient than going to your bank, standing in a long line, waiting to be served.

Despite these benefits, there's always a risk of exposure to all kinds of attacks when conducting financial transactions online. Without the right security mechanisms in place, you could not only waste your time and money, but you could lose everything online, including your confidential information like contacts and addresses.

From password managers to biometric verification and two-step authentication methods, there are many solutions for protecting your secure data online. You must also remember the basics. For example, never share your information with anyone, keep your personal data private, and only use authentic websites. If you are running any software, make sure it is always updated to the current version in order to limit your vulnerability.

## Investment Awareness

People miss investment opportunities all the time, not because they don't know about them, but because of information overload from different outlets. You need the right information at the right time to make the right investment choices. You may receive this information on time, but fail to act on it because it got lost in all the other notifications you receive on your devices.

To avoid that struggle, you can create information filters to prioritize important investment information that affects your portfolio. One way to successfully achieve this is to use news aggregation programs to track news stories about investments you are interested in. Most of these platforms today use different machine learning algorithms to match your investment needs with precise news headlines so you never have to waste time searching the internet for what you need.

## Affordable Investment Access

For a long time, retail investors have been put off certain investments because of high commissions and other fees. This isn't the case anymore. Many investment firms have leveraged the benefits of internet access and drastically reduced the commissions charged on their services, especially for those who trade securities and other financial instruments.

Many brokers used to charge rates that would be considered extortion in the financial markets today. The internet opened up access to investments for everyone. This created room for more competitive pricing and attractive products for investors. Eventually, as the competition increased, brokers and financial service providers had to either innovate, offer lower fees, or do both to stay ahead and appeal to their customers. This explains why today we have lots of discount brokers offering amazing, yet affordable services to investors.

The bottom line is that the internet has shifted the dynamics of investment power from brokers and investment firms to customers. This primarily comes down to the ease with which you can access information, and how fast you can implement changes to your portfolio based on that information.

Even though technology has already had a profound impact on the investment world, there's still so much untapped potential as we embrace evolving markets and investment products. For example, today, people have invested billions of dollars in cryptocurrencies all over the world, yet there was a time when these assets didn't exist, let alone the thought of people trading in them. The secret to winning the investment race through technology is to stay informed, and use all the tools and systems you have to your advantage.

## Impact of Technologies in the Trucking Business

Earlier we talked about the importance of not just staying in the trucking and transportation business, but running a profitable and sustainable operation over the long term. One sure way to achieve this is by embracing the technological advancements around you. Do that, and you will run a successful business in the industry for a long time.

Advanced technologies have influenced progress in the trucking industry and helped many entrepreneurs identify growth opportunities and niche segments that were previously untapped. Let's discuss some significant technological functions that will have an impact on your trucking business:

## 1. Improved Customer Service

One of the best things about technology in the trucking and transportation business is that it's helped to not only streamline business processes, but improve customer service. Task automation is one of the smart approaches you can implement to understand and engage your customers better. By addressing their behaviors and preferences, you can easily improve your customer retention rates.

## 2. Data and Decision Making

All programs and systems used in the trucking business collect and store a lot of data, from customer interactions to order and fleet management systems. Most older systems could only collect data. However, modern systems collect, analyze, and process the data. This enables us to make important decisions using the processed information in real-time, like planning your routes and scheduling orders on time.

## 3. Analytics and Optimization

As businesses evolve, one-size-fits-all methods become unreliable and unproductive. Instead, successful businesses use analytical techniques to optimize their business operations. These are techniques that are unique to your business and circumstances. With systems like Google Optimizer and Frontline, you have access to innovative technologies, helping you streamline your business in real-time.

## 4. Machine Learning

Machine learning is a subset of artificial intelligence that can help you automate many routines or repetitive tasks, especially those that involve a lot of data analysis and processing. The good news is that business systems today produce and use a lot of data, which provide good training models for machine learning algorithms. Everyday tasks like driver allocation and optimizing fuel stops along the driver's route can be automated instead of attending to them on a case-by-case basis. You can even use chatbots to enhance your interaction with customers, by keeping them informed in real-time through GPS data.

## 5. Cloud Computing

Many small and medium-sized businesses struggle to implement innovative technologies in their business models because of limited access to supporting business infrastructure, or they simply can't afford them. Cloud computing has changed all that by making software solutions easily available and affordable. Instead of paying for expensive machine learning solutions, for example, small businesses can get them affordably through cloud service providers like Azure. One of the benefits of cloud computing is that it drastically reduces the cost of obtaining and using crucial programs, systems, and business applications.

## 6. Freight Tracking and Management

Real-time freight tracking puts you in a better position to understand the whereabouts of your drivers and trucks, and, more importantly, to provide accurate updates to customers. You don't have to keep them on the phone waiting while you try to contact your drivers, who may be unreachable while on the road for various valid reasons.

Apart from tracking, we have lots of innovative ways to manage freight. Cloud-based freight matching, for example, helps to improve your productivity by proper time and fuel management. There are different kinds of freight matching programs you can use to reduce empty miles by connecting with other shippers and brokers.

Ultimately, we cannot ignore the role or impact of technologies in the trucking and transportation business. Learning about new technologies, and how other businesses are implementing technologies in their operations, helps you understand how to stay profitable and run a successful and self-sustaining trucking business.

## Useful Trucking Technologies

To succeed in any investment, it's imperative that you stay updated with the technology trends unique to that sector. For example, if you buy stock in a company like Ford, you'll need to pay attention to advanced technologies in the auto industry, the moves that electric vehicle companies like Tesla are making, and how they affect not just Ford, but the auto industry in general. This is how you stay ahead of the curve.

In the trucking and transportation business, the same concept applies. One of the areas where emerging technologies have contributed significantly towards profitability in this sector is in enhanced safety and security. This business is about more than moving cargo or people from one place to another; it's also about the people involved, the processes, and the equipment, all of which benefit from safety and security in one way or another.

Ultimately, three areas where technological interventions make your business better and more profitable are: safer business environment, more efficient operations, and reduced costs. Let's briefly mention some useful apps that will have a profound impact on your trucking business:

## 1. Collision Mitigation Systems

These systems are designed to detect precarious or uncertain moving and stationary objects and warn the driver of the impending danger of collision. Once you receive the alert, you can activate cruise control or brake to keep a safe distance from the imminent hazard. This will save you time, money, and unnecessary repair costs.

## 2. Digital Freight Matching Apps

These apps meet your revenue maximization needs by connecting carriers and shippers. You can think of digital freight matching apps as the Uber of trucking. They eliminate the struggle of looking for customers and connect you to a ready market depending on your route, date of availability and the capacity of your trucks. This is a good workaround for empty miles. uShip, Uber freight and Convoy are some apps you may want to consider.

## 3. Driver Scorecards

Drivers are extremally crucial to your success in the trucking and transportation business, so it's important that you take their performance seriously. Ideally, driver scorecards are all about tracking and mapping driver behavior while they are on the road to recognize top performers and to promptly respond to safety issues when they arise.

From this information, it's easier to identify drivers who need more training or retraining, those who handle difficult routes better, and so on. Since you learn so much about your drivers, this can be a good tool for rewarding exceptional talent.

## 4. Dynamic Routing Apps

At face value, these are GPS apps. You may be wondering why you would invest in a GPS app while they come free on your phone. Well, the secret is in the name. The average GPS app may be ineffective where traffic jams, road repairs, and bad weather are concerned. With dynamic routing, all these possibilities are factored in, helping you find better routes instantly. Apps like CoPilot provide real-time routing suggestions which eventually reduce delays on the road, and the app will give you the best route based on the height (or clearance) of your vehicle as well.

## 5. Electronic Logging Devices

The Federal Motor Carrier Safety Administration (FMCSA) has strict guidelines for driver safety and compliance in the trucking and transportation industry. One of these is the use of electronic logging devices to monitor trucking operations. These systems, together with other safety software, provide insight into the overall driving experience. They log everything, including how long the driver is on the road, location, mileage covered, speed, and the truck engine. From this information, you can easily tell whether your drivers are overworked, if there are difficult routes, and it even shows the performance of your trucks on certain routes as well.

## 6. Fleet Management Apps

Fleet management apps build on the gains made by driver scorecards. Driver scorecards are ideal for individual driver assessment. However, if you have more drivers, fleet management apps will be most effective. Some useful information you will derive from these apps includes the average cost per mile, service costs, fuel consumption levels, hours, and mileage covered.

Ideally, fleet management apps help you identify points of inefficiency in your fleet and address them right away. For example, you can automate routine service scheduling for your trucks once they complete a set number of miles. Fleetio and Simply Fleet are good examples that many drivers use.

## 7. Forward-Looking Camera Systems

These cameras are crucial when assessing damage for insurance claims. Generally, most people assume that truck drivers are often at fault in the event of an accident. This is a common assumption of fatigue because of their notoriously long hours on the road, even if the truck driver wasn't at fault. The cameras capture events as they unfold, which makes it easier to plead your driver's innocence and to avoid unnecessary costs.

## 8. Fuel Price Apps

No one feels the impact of fuel price changes like trucking companies. Your trucks are on the road more than the average driver, making fuel consumption a major expense in your business. Fuel price apps help you save money by comparing pump prices along your route. Apart from that, some apps also identify stations where you'll pay less taxes on fuel, or where your trucks can fit into a certain station given their ground clearance.

## 9. GPS Apps

For most car drivers, the average GPS app is a good enough guide for navigation. However, truck drivers need more than that. Truck drivers need additional information like suggestions for resting points, or roads that are specifically inaccessible to trucks. This is what you get from

GPS apps like Tracker Path—routing information unique to truck driver needs.

## 10. Platooning Apps

Truck platooning is a coordinated system where two or more trucks use automated driving support systems to travel in a convoy. The trucks make the journey, or parts of it, together, keeping a close distance throughout the platooning section of that trip. This coordination helps to counter the adverse effects of wind resistance, overcome traffic issues, especially on a motorway, and it improves the efficiency of your trucks on the road.

## 11. Telematics

Telematics is the use of vehicle technologies like wireless devices, onboard diagnostics, GPS systems and other sensors to record and transmit crucial data about the trucks like location, speed, maintenance schedules, and driver and truck activity on the road to understand the behavior of your trucks in real-time. These apps help you track your cargo throughout the journey, and can also be useful when planning your vehicle scheduling times.

## 12. Vehicle Maintenance Apps

Apps like Fleet Rabbit are useful for scheduling regular inspections and maintenance for your trucks. Without these apps, you'd have to perform these tasks manually, which might not be so efficient and will eventually cost you a lot of money. By automating such routine tasks, you eliminate a lot of unnecessary repetitive work and focus on running the business.

It's clear to see the important role that technology plays in ensuring you run a smooth and profitable trucking and transportation business. Everything from getting shipping loads to managing your fleet and drivers can be streamlined with the right technological interventions and tools.

If you've ever wondered how some of the big trucking companies stay ahead of the curve, this is the secret. It is a competitive industry, and you must adapt and keep refining your business process and models by leveraging the power of emerging technologies where it's most needed. Technology has definitely changed the course of business, and all you have to do is identify what works for you and implement it the right way.

## Checklist and CDL Minded Approach

There are different types of apps and software solutions available on the market that you can use to streamline your trucking business. We discussed quite a number of categories to help you understand their value. This checklist reviews the different types of apps available. Note that some of these solutions are free, while others are premium products that require a monthly subscription, or purchasing the solution upfront. Also, as technology constantly changes over time, some apps may be outdated or unavailable, so choose one that you can easily use and remember to factor the costs into your decision-making.

| Task | Examples of apps and software solutions available | Notes |
|---|---|---|
| Collision management systems | F-CAM, Safe Drive Systems, Samsara, Torsa | |
| Freight matching | uShip, Uber Freight, Convoy, DAT Trucker, ITS Trucker | |
| Driver scorecard | DriverApp, Transflo Mobile, KeepTruckin TruckerPath | |
| Dynamic routing | Copilot, RouteSavvy, Badger Maps, MapQuest | |
| Fleet management | Simply Fleet, Fleetio, Teletrac Navman ClearPathGPS, Rhino Fleet Tracking | |
| Electronic logging device | Garmin eLog, Gorilla Safety, Omnitracs, GPS Trackit, Matrack | |
| Forward-looking camera | Garmin Dash Cam Blackvue, Zenfoxx, Redtiger Dash Cam | |
| Fuel price apps | Fuelbook, Gas Buddy, Trucker Path | |
| GPS | Copilot, Waze, PTV Navigator, Sygic | |
| Platooning | Geotab, Peloton Technology | |
| Telematics solutions | Switchboard, Webfleet, Nextraq, Linxup, Brickhouse Security | |
| Vehicle maintenance | Fleet Maintenance Pro, RTA Fleet, Fleet Harmony, EMDECS, FleetCommander | |

## CHAPTER 7

# THE FINANCIAL WALKTHROUGH OF SUCCESS

Y ou've done everything right so far, and are on course to set up your trucking business. Now, let's discuss the one area where many people get it wrong—finances. Even if you are passionate about trucks and trucking, this is a business, and business is about money. If you don't figure your finances out, things may not work out so well for you.

Just as you made the right investment decisions, you must also now make the right financial decisions to support your business idea. One thing you can bank on is that the trucking business has been a promising industry with lots of opportunities for many years. At the moment, the massive scale of vacancies and driver shortages means that you can set up and start making money right away. Even if you don't have all the money you need right away, we'll discuss some useful financing tips to help you get your business on the road.

## Is Trucking Still a Profitable Business?

The year 2020 and part of 2021 were rough for everyone. The Covid pandemic was ravaging economies all over the world. With governments imposing lockdowns to try to control the spread of the virus, the trucking industry, like all other sectors, was dealt severe blows. However, with vaccine drives and other protocols observed, many governments have relaxed and even done away with the restrictions, a move seen as the revival that many businesses had been hoping for.

The good news is that the trucking industry, like most other industries, is bouncing back and things are looking up. One possible reason for this bounce back, as we mentioned earlier, is the fact that trucking is the backbone of every industry in our economy. Therefore, as soon as the lockdowns ceased and people started getting their lives back on track, trucking activities picked up naturally.

Of course, this isn't to say that everything will be smooth, but the progress trajectory is impressive. We are still struggling with driver shortages, which are limiting the industry's capacity to operate at its full potential. Things get even trickier when we consider the challenge of increased demand from consumers. This, however, also means that there's more work available in trucking than the available truckers can handle. If you were looking for a reason to believe trucking is still profitable, this is it.

What can you do to succeed in this industry and earn the kind of profits that will help you build your trucking empire? Here are some quick-fire tips to guide you:

First, realize that the trucking industry is so wide, there are lots of opportunities for everyone. Therefore, pick a niche that works for you, research it well, and find out what works for your customers. This will also be a good opportunity to learn about the operating costs and fueling strategies you can implement to save on fuel costs.

Next, success in this industry depends on networking and relationships. Talk to other shippers and build relationships. Some of the useful tips you will learn from these relationships include figuring out an appropriate dispatch system, managing customer credit, and automated billing and compliance systems.

Finally, profitability comes down to your product pricing. Your pricing can either get you new customers or chase the regular ones away. Research more about the current market prices and the contributing factors. Once you can set optimal prices that work for both your customers and your business, focus on your cash flow position. Cash flow management means ensuring that you always have money around to keep the business going, even if you are yet to be paid by your customers.

Whether trucking becomes a profitable investment for you or not depends on how you effectively manage the business. It takes a lot of diligent financial management and proper planning to make things work round the clock. More importantly, make sure you understand all the costs involved in running the business, from the initial costs of setting up the business to the cost of insurance, so that nothing comes up as a surprise to you.

## The Cost of Doing Business

One of the most rewarding ways to invest in the trucking and transportation business is as an owner-operator. This is quite an advantageous position because you have so much control over the kind of work you do, and the type of customers you work for. To succeed as an owner-operator, here are some of the important costs you must learn to manage:

- Initial Cost

This is simply the amount of money you need to set up your business. On average, most people invest around $10,000 to start their operation, though you can still get the ball rolling with around $6,000. Note that this doesn't include the cost of equipment. Also, some prices will fluctuate depending on where, when, and how you start your operation. Note that prices and cost of living change over time so be sure to plan ahead and save as much as possible.

- Fixed and Variable Costs

This classification of costs will help you understand where most of your money goes. Fixed costs are generally consistent throughout the life of your business. They include annual permits, insurance, and taxes. On the other hand, variable costs are mostly unpredictable, and are influenced by factors beyond your control. Repair costs, fuel costs, and fines are common variable costs you'll need to plan for.

- U.S. DOT Number

You'll need a U.S. Department of Transportation (DOT) number, which at the time of this publication, cost $300. Be sure to check the DOT Website in your area to find out how much a DOT number costs as prices change over time.

- Business Registration

It's illegal to operate without a business registration. The cost to register your business depends on your location. However, you can plan for around $500.

- Unified Carrier Registration

This is a mandatory program for companies or individuals driving commercial vehicles to register in any participating states annually, and the cost depends on the number of trucks in your fleet.

- Buying a Truck

You can either buy a new or used truck. Each of these has its pros and cons, but always remember that the most important thing is to own a truck that's in excellent condition for your needs.

Beyond the cost of buying the truck, consider the repair and maintenance costs as well, and make sure it's within a manageable range. For used trucks, a good rule of thumb is to make sure the truck has no more than five years on the road, with an engine that's covered no more than 600,000 miles. Of course, there are other important factors that you'll need to look at before buying a used truck, not just those two. Depending on your needs and budget, expect to spend at least $15,000 on a truck, with an open limit depending on the additional features the truck may have.

- Insurance

This is a mandatory cost and you may not be able to legally operate your trucks without it. The cost of insurance depends on several factors, including the driver's experience, age of the truck, location, and the type of cargo you'll be working with. Note that the annual cost of insurance is charged per truck. You may be able to reduce your annual insurance premiums by installing electronic logging devices recommended, and often, required by the FMCSA.

- Licenses and Endorsements

Once you obtain your CDL, you can also pursue endorsements to allow your permits to transport special cargo, or operate special trucks. Note that you have to pay for each endorsement.

Other than the costs we've already discussed, you'll also need business cards, a website, and a professional social media presence. Therefore, set aside around $5,000 for marketing and advertising your business, and miscellaneous expenses.

## Equipment Financing

From the cost breakdown in the previous section, it's clear that you'll need a lot of money to set up your trucking operation. If you have that money saved, or you can get it from your friends or family members, you'll be good to go. However, if you don't have those options, equipment financing may be best for you.

Equipment financing is a loan or lease agreement that helps you buy or borrow equipment and other physical assets for your business. There are different types of equipment financing agreements that you can consider, depending on your needs. You will only be approved for an amount that your business can afford to pay, considering the condition of the equipment and the market price.

Before you do, understand that in an equipment financing agreement, the physical asset you obtain acts as collateral for your loan. Therefore, if you default, the lender can repossess the asset. Because of this arrangement, you may also qualify for financing if your credit isn't perfect. However, your interest rates may be higher.

Compared to all other types of financing available to you, equipment financing may be the most cost-effective option for funding your business without using your own money. Note that some lenders may require a down payment of up to 20% if the asset you wish to finance is considered a risky purchase, especially with a high rate of depreciation.

This form of financing is useful under the following circumstances:

- when you need money urgently

- if you only need to buy equipment

- if you don't have any collateral for a loan

Of all the financing options available, this approach offers the most flexibility, especially when business picks up and you need to expand to match the growing capacity. You could also enjoy more tax benefits through equipment financing than buying the equipment upfront. This is because the equipment isn't considered an asset in your accounting books, but an expense.

The financing terms are fairly straightforward and predictable, so it's easier to manage and budget for it each month. This allows you to plan for and spread your payments out even years ahead.

Another good reason to consider equipment financing is that it doesn't lock you out of other financing opportunities. Since the equipment is the collateral for its loan, you can still use other options available to get more financing if you need to.

Lenders will consider your overall business income and expense position, your cash flow, any debts you are servicing, and your credit score to determine the amount of money you can be approved for. Your experience in the industry may also help your case. For example, many lenders offer this service to truckers who have been in the business for at least two years.

Apart from that, they'll also want to know more about the equipment you want to buy. Let's say you want to buy a truck, for example. Is it new or used? Are you buying from a private contact or a licensed seller? For a used truck, how many miles has it covered? This information helps them estimate the real value of the truck.

Since there are many lenders offering this service, take your time to research and understand the required cost that comes with it so you can pick a lender you can reasonably afford. Lending terms vary from one lender to the next, but the terms are typically 1-5 years, depending on the type of equipment.

With this information, your next step is to find the right financing strategy. Visit different banks and learn about their offers. Note that though banks generally have good rates, their requirements tend to be stricter. You can also consider online lenders, who usually offer competitive rates too. Some vendors also have in-house financing options, where you obtain the equipment from them, but they retain ownership while you use and pay for the equipment in installments.

## Planning the Investment

There's a lot that goes into planning and managing your business and investments. One of the most important activities is budgeting. A budget helps you do more than just allocate your money for different activities, it also helps you understand where your money goes. Whether you are on a shoestring budget or you have all the money you need to run the trucking business, a budget will always come in handy.

To support your budgeting needs, here are five important strategies that will help you plan well for your business finances:

- Save! Save! Save!

This is probably one of the oldest financial tips in the world. Saving ensures you have extra money when you need it. In business, like in life, there will always be unexpected surprises from time to time. If you don't save, each of these surprises will be an emergency situation that forces you to either take a loan that you can't afford in the first place, or cut back on other important parts of your business. The last thing you would want is to dip into your business money to address emergency issues. Therefore, have an emergency fund in place. It doesn't matter how little you save; anything is better than nothing.

- Tax Refunds and Bonuses

This is another source of earnings that many people never think of. If you file your taxes correctly, you may realize instances where you are eligible for tax refunds. Your accountant can assist with this if tax accounting isn't something you'd enjoy doing. The refunds, bonuses or discounts you receive in the course of business should go towards boosting your savings or investment fund. Other similar sources of "free money" include cash-back rewards and loyalty programs on your credit cards.

- Talk to the Experts

It's good to accept that you may not always know everything, and more importantly, that from time to time it's okay to ask for help. On financial matters, many people would do so much better if they just took a moment to speak to professionals. From a financial advisor to an accountant, there are many experts out there who can help you understand your financial position better. Your bank, for example, has quite a number of these professionals, who will mostly assist you for free—it is their work, after all.

- Alternative Investments

Your primary investment is your trucking business. However, it is financially wise never to put all your eggs in one basket. This is an investment concept known as diversification. Spread your money around in multiple income-producing assets. This way, if something bad ever happens to your trucking business, your business will not be completely scrambled or crack under pressure. Scrambled eggs may be awesome, but no one likes them off the floor.

Other kinds of investments you can consider include stocks, mutual funds, bonds, 401(k) plans, investing in real estate, cryptocurrency, and so on. The financial market is full of investment opportunities, you just need to know where to look.

Hint—this is another instance where talking to the experts will come in handy!

- Understand Your Finances

Does your financial position match your ambition? We all have some financial goals or targets we wish to achieve, but our financial situation may be holding us back. Understand how much money you are working with. Assess your total income against your expenses, and review your budget and savings to figure out how much money you can invest. For this assessment to be effective, you must be reasonable and brutally honest with yourself about your finances.

With these strategies, you can then come up with an elaborate financial plan to fire up the engines on your investment journey.

## Checklist and CDL Minded Approach

Your financing approach plays an important role in the way you run your business. At this point, you should have already spoken to different lenders or financial partners, if necessary, and settled on the best one considering your financial status, credit rating, and more importantly, the amount of money you will need. You can keep track of your financial progress in your CDL transportation and trucking business with the following checklist:

| Activity | Tasks involved | Complete? |
| --- | --- | --- |
| Business capital | As per our discussion, you should prepare between $6,000 and $10,000 to start. Even better if you have more. | |
| Registration costs | This should meet the cost of licenses, permits, endorsements, and membership to any trucking organizations that may help you get a footing in the industry.<br><br>Notable expenses include DOT Number, business registration, and getting your Unified Carrier Registration. | |
| Insurance | Research the best insurance providers in the industry for your trucks, and for your business if you are setting up a physical office. | |
| Truck purchase | Revisit truck acquisition plan. Are you getting a new or used truck? Are you buying or leasing the truck? You've researched well, so refine your options, finalize the plan, and get yourself a truck. | |

| Business financing | Go to your preferred lender and finalize arrangements for invoice processing, and any other issue that may require their assistance. | |
| --- | --- | --- |
| Savings plan | Set up your emergency savings fund, and automate your savings process. | |

# CHAPTER 8

# STREAMLINING THE CLERICAL JOB

There's more to running a successful and profitable trucking business than driving trucks and moving cargo from one point to the next. While this is the core of your business, you need other professional services to streamline your operation and make it easier to handle the trucking and shipping bit.

Let's face it; this is a money business. It's not just about how many shipments you handle every week or month, but also about how much money is coming in or moving out of your business. While it may be awesome to stay on top of things and handle the finances on your own, it could get overwhelming, and that's where the cracks start to show in your business. Instead of taking that risk, why not bring in the experts?

CPAs and financial advisors, for example, will offer greater insight into the financial position of your business. You can learn so much from them, and your business will be better with their input. It's not only about saving time by outsourcing financial or clerical work, but also about using their skills to identify and solve financial problems in your business. Where investments are concerned, you cannot afford to overlook or ignore things like taxes, risk factors, or anything else that involves your time, energy and money.

## Advantages of Hiring a CPA

There's a reason why people like financial advisors and CPAs are referred to as professionals or experts. From experience, they have a unique set of skills for identifying financial issues that most people would not be able to see at a glance. This is why even financial companies that have lots of these experts on their payroll still seek external professional services on a consultancy basis to help them figure out anything that their internal experts may have overlooked.

Hiring a CPA doesn't have to be expensive. With proper research, you'll definitely find a CPA whose services are within a range you can afford. Below, let's mention five important reasons why you should hire a professional to help you streamline your finances:

- Tax Purposes

CPAs understand taxes better than you do unless, of course, you are a CPA yourself, in which case, you might still need someone to look through your tax documents in case you missed anything.

Tax compliance is mandatory for every business. From federal tax laws to state and local tax laws, you must always pay your taxes on time and the right way. The role of a CPA isn't just to make sure you do that, but also to help you find opportunities to reduce your tax liability. If the IRA ever needs to audit your finances, your CPA can help you defend your position, proving that you've filed your tax returns promptly, and your tax liability is correct.

- Budgeting

One aspect of budgeting that can help you manage a successful business is knowing where to cut costs, and where to increase your investment. By analyzing your previous expenditure, which is the amount of funds you're spending, a CPA can easily recommend areas where you can eliminate or reduce spending, and use that money for additional investment, or savings. The CPA may also help you realize how much you can save by outsourcing some tasks instead of having a full-time employee.

- Legal Compliance

As a registered business, there are several authorities that require compliance from you in order for you to retain your permits or licenses. Naturally, you may forget some of them, given all the work you have to do to keep the business running. Failure to comply may result in having your permits and licenses revoked. A CPA's work is to make sure this never happens. They'll remind you of, or make renewal applications and submit payments due, on time.

- Forecasting and Future Planning

Finally, one area where you'll greatly benefit from working with a professional CPA is their forecasting skills. Using their knowledge of corporate finance, financial reporting, accounting, taxation, and other financial roles, a CPA can provide more insight into your finances, potential investments, and how changes in some economic factors may affect your business. With this information, they can advise you on strategic steps you can take to protect your business.

## Questions to Ask Your CPA

Before you hire a CPA, you must ensure they don't just meet your budget needs but are also capable of addressing your financial needs. Note that a CPA is by profession a general advisor. However, you need someone with special skills or knowledge and experience in the trucking industry, especially if you are an owner-operator. Here are some important issues your CPA should address to meet your requirements:

- On Per Diem Rates

The CPA should guarantee you up to 80% of $69 a day in the continental U.S. Anyone who offers you 50% is referring to the general standard that applies everywhere. You need trucking-specific rates, not general rates.

Assuming you are claiming per diem for 300 days a year, 80% of $69 gives you $16,560, while 50% of $69 gives you $10,350. You'll be losing $6,210 in tax write-offs every year if you use a general CPA.

On the same note, if your spouse or anyone without a CDL rides in the truck with you, but performs other tasks apart from driving, like loading, dispatch, or bookkeeping, they can claim per diem rates of 50% of $69 per day.

- On Standard Mileage Deductions

Since the IRS considers your truck as a vehicle not intended for personal use, you can't use the standard mileage method. All you can do is claim actual expenses incurred and involved in your trucking operation. Doing the contrary may land you in trouble during an IRS audit.

- On Accompaniments

If you are training a student driver, you'll mostly pay for some bills, especially meals throughout the journey. You can claim these deductions. General CPAs will ask you not to, because they assume that the business reimburses such expenses. If that's not your case, it's okay to claim the deductions.

Other than your student driver, you may have your pet in the cab area to keep you company on those long trips. There isn't much clarity or a consensus on this matter, but with some guidelines, your CPA should help you claim deductions on your pet's expenses, especially if you consider them a part of your security system.

- On Paperwork

How does your CPA handle business documentation? Now, this is important because you'd want someone who is proactive. Ideally, you need someone you can send documents to instantly. There are lots of apps and system solutions that allow this, making your work easier when handling receipts, invoices, and any other documents. This also means you have access to the system 24/7 throughout the year.

It's not just for paperwork that you need availability throughout; your trucking business is in operation throughout the year, so it's only fair that you should hire a CPA who will be available to you in a heart-beat. Some CPAs mostly offer their consulting services around the time you need to file tax returns, which ends up being too much work. Instead, get someone who is with you every step of the way.

- Cost

Next, agree on the CPA's costing structure, because this will be a re-current expense in your books. Some professionals charge by the hour, while others bill you a flat weekly or monthly rate, depending on the amount of work they do for you, or whichever agreement you settle on. The best solution here will depend on your business structure and overall financial needs.

Finally, remember that the CPA is there to work for you, and help you improve your business. For that reason, remind them of your business goals in order to help them align their work with your business objectives.

## Questions to Ask Your Financial Advisor

Like CPAs, it would greatly benefit your business to work with a financial advisor. As there are quite a number of them in the market, you should vet and choose your options carefully, so you don't end up hiring someone who won't create time for you. Going by the nature of their profession, most financial advisors are generally busy.

Some financial advisors are independent contractors, while others are company employees. With that in mind, you need someone whose focus isn't just reaching their revenue targets, but a desire to help you make the right financial moves. Here are some pointers to help you find the right financial advisor:

- Professional Qualifications

It doesn't matter whether your business is a year old or ten, when you hire a professional, you should get your money's worth for professional services. Discuss their licenses, experience in the industry, permits where applicable, and qualifications. You may also want to know more about the kind of investments they have or even the types of clients they've worked with in their portfolios.

- Professional Services

Like CPAs, there are many advisory services that fall under a financial advisor's department. However, some, or most of those services may not be relevant to you. You don't need general advisory services. You need someone who has experience with trucking operations, and has in-depth knowledge of how the industry works. That is someone who'll most likely understand your frustrations and challenges easily. This may also be a good time to find out what services they don't offer.

- Costs and Expenses

How much will their advisory services cost you, and are their fees negotiable? Discuss the frequency of your payments, and the structure of your payments to or from customers. Be sure not to underestimate any of your costs.

- Preferred Investment Approach

Seeing that this is someone who may be handling your investments on your behalf, how much approval do they need for your transactions? What is their preferred level of involvement in your financial affairs? What if you are not comfortable with it? Can they work with your terms?

How frequently do they trade? What do they think of your preferred investments, or what kind of investments do they think you should avoid altogether? Ask them to describe an ideal investment portfolio mix that they would recommend to you right away, even before looking at your finances.

- Performance Expectations

Before you hire a financial advisor, they should give you some guarantees on the performance expectations. Given a certain investment amount, say $10,000, what returns can you expect annually in a year, five, or ten years? Of course, no one can predict what will happen in the financial markets, but from their experience, your advisor should be able to give you a rough estimate of what to expect. Note that in the financial markets, none of this is guaranteed to happen as they say it should, so keep an open mind.

- Additional Account Services

There's a good chance you'll probably recommend their services to your close friends and family members if you like their work. How do they handle this? Will they charge you extra for this? Do you get a discount?

Lastly, one of the most important services you need from a financial advisor is financial planning. Talk to your advisor about your retirement plans, or your ideas about the financial position you need to attain in a few years. Given those insights, listen to their plan on how to get from where you are to where you intend to be.

Your financial advisor is a shoulder to lean on, your guide, someone who will leave a lasting impact on your investment plans, and financial well-being in the future. Don't leave anything off the table, ask them anything that comes to mind, despite how insignificant you think it may be.

## CPA Versus Enrolled Agent. Who Should I Hire?

While it may be great to find a financial advisor or a CPA who can help you understand how your money works in the trucking business, they are not the only ones who can assist. You may actually need an Enrolled Agent (EA) instead. This is a tax professional who can assist you on tax matters involving the IRS, including appeals, audits, and collections. In their capacity, they can also provide professional advice on tax matters.

The procedure to become an EA is quite rigorous, and the agents must also pass a background check while applying to the IRS. The EA is a special designation in that the tax professional must meet the ethical requirements outlined by the Department of the Treasury, and commit to completing 72 hours of continuing education every three years.

The professional body to which most EAs enroll, the National Association of Enrolled Agents, maintains the highest standards for ethics, and guidelines for continuing education. Therefore, if your EA belongs to this organization, there's a good chance you are working with one of the best in the industry.

So, who should you work with between a CPA and an EA? To answer this question, let's first take a look at their roles. As a state-licensed accounting expert, a Certified Public Accountant (CPA) can assist you in different capacities, such as tax consulting, auditing, accountancy, business advisory services, forensic accountancy, or financial planning.

Most CPAs are members of the American Institute of CPAs, an organization with a high code of professional conduct. Therefore, like EAs, it's good to find out if your CPA is a member or not, as such professional groups uphold the highest standards of ethics and professionalism. Besides, while the requirements for retaining a CPA license may vary between states, all CPAs are required to complete 40 hours of continuing education each year.

From our analysis, CPAs and EAs are both professionals who maintain the highest ethical standards in their work. The main difference in their services is that while CPAs can offer taxation and other services, an EA's specialty is taxation. Their services, therefore, will depend on the work you need.

An EA, for example, is a valuable asset if you ever have an issue with the IRS. This is anything from an audit, collection issue or any other problem that may arise with the IRS. Besides, some EAs were probably IRS agents before they branched off as independent contractors, so they have the best knowledge of the workings of the IRS, and will be your best choice on IRS matters.

Even though EAs may not be able to prepare and provide audited financial statements like CPAs do, they can help you with everything concerning taxation, from preparation to planning, both for your business and for personal needs. You can, therefore, consult them for any tax-related statements that will be used when preparing your tax returns.

CPAs can also help you on IRS matters, just like EAs. A CPA who specializes in tax preparation can also assist with accounting, financial planning, and tax planning. They'll mostly handle any financial task you may need help with. A CPA should be able to advise on areas where you can reduce your tax bill, deductions, and credits you qualify for.

There's not much of a difference in what an EA and a CPA can do to help your business, especially if your emphasis is on taxation. The EA exam, however, is quite comprehensive and deals mostly with the federal tax system and ethical issues. It is common to find EAs with clients who are CPAs because the licensing test for CPAs is quite diverse, with only one section dedicated to taxation. The EA exam, on the other hand, is all about taxation, with only one section reserved for ethics.

In summary, the argument here isn't to suggest that one of these professionals is better than the other. They can both offer valuable business and tax consultancy services. However, the fact that someone is a CPA doesn't necessarily guarantee that they will have the tax skills or experience you need for your business, or for your personal tax needs.

## Checklist and CDL Minded Approach

The role of an accountant is one of the most important ones in your business, besides trucking. Their work is to make sure that your money is spent the right way, and, more importantly, offer support and advice on all financial matters so you never have a nasty run-in with the IRS. Whether you opt for a CPA, a Financial Advisor, or an Enrolled Agent is up to you. However, since whoever you choose will primarily work on your accounting books, use this checklist to help you select the right one for your business.

| Assessment | What to look for | Complete? Yes or No |
| --- | --- | --- |
| Industry experience | Experience is important because you need someone who can guide you. Remember, you are not just looking at their professional experience in accounting, but experience in the trucking industry. | |
| Startup experience | Does the accounting professional have some experience in working with startups? As this is your first time in the business, you need solutions that are relevant to your status, and not generalized solutions. | |

| | | |
|---|---|---|
| Fees | How much will their services cost? Are their fees negotiable? Do you get bonuses or discounts for referring other startup truckers to them? | |
| Availability | Since you are just setting up your operation and don't really know how frequently you will need their services, how available are they? Trucking goes on throughout the year, so your accountant should also be reasonably available for you on demand. | |
| Security | Do they have a secure platform for sharing documents? Your invoices, receipts, and other financial documents include your and your customers' information, which should be protected through appropriate encryption methods. | |
| Tech solutions | It's a tech-savvy world, so the person handling your accounts should be well-informed about software solutions for accounting, like QuickBooks, and be ready to teach you how to use them so that you are always on the same page. | |

# CHAPTER 9

# BACK TO THE FUTURE

**W**hen investing in any business opportunity, it's always a good idea to think of what the future holds for that industry in general. You wouldn't want to put your money in a business that may become obsolete in the future. This is one area where the trucking industry has always had an advantage. Every single product you own or interact with right now was once in a truck being delivered from one point to another. Even when you are done with the things you use and throw them away, they'll still end up in a truck. So, trucks are there at every step in the life cycle of everything you use.

So, what does the future hold for trucking businesses? Answering this question will also answer another important question that many beginners worry about—*am I making the right decision?*

The fact is that the future prospect for the trucking industry is bright. This is the important lesson we learned during the Covid pandemic. At a time when most economies almost ground to a halt, there was increasing demand for products, both at the consumer and enterprise level. Since then, companies all over the world have been busy restructuring their operations, with some moving to full remote working models, while others have switched to hybrid working models. The implication here is that there'll be more demand for equipment and other products that fit these living and working conditions.

More people working at home also means that people now have more freedom to do things at home that they never had time to. Introduce the growing reliance on e-commerce, and you can understand why the delivery sector of the trucking industry has made a lot of money since the pandemic. These trends will continue in the future, which loosely translates to more dependence on the trucking industry. This further strengthens the point that the trucking industry is in dire need of more truckers, drivers and owner-operators in order to fill the massive shortage that has plagued the industry for many years. If you were still looking for a sign to invest in the CDL trucking industry, this is it.

## Trucking and the Pandemic

Even though the trucking industry didn't completely grind to a halt during the Covid pandemic, it did suffer some challenges, like every other industry. The good news is that during this difficult time, trucks were still needed. If anything, demand for trucking was even higher. The pandemic highlighted just how much the economy needed the trucking industry.

The sector lost many workers, not just the drivers behind the wheels, but also management and administrative staff who help the drivers meet their deliverables on a daily basis. This was also the time when we endured a global fuel crisis, further hurting supply chains that were already struggling with the effects of the pandemic. The unfortunate situation in the trucking industry is that these challenges struck right at the heart of the trucking business. The good news is that we somehow managed to navigate through this crisis, and the industry has been on a recovery trajectory now more than ever. Even more important are the lessons we learned from it.

As a CDL minded investor, there are several factors you should consider when investing your money in the transportation and trucking industry. Remember that your end goal is to run a successful business that prioritizes safety, operational efficiency, and protecting the environment while making passive, active and residual income on your investments.

Moving forward, it's clear that timely delivery will always be a priority. This is actually one of the lessons from the pandemic that stressed how valuable trucking and transportation is to the economy. Of course, a shortage of truckers means that trucking companies may struggle to meet all delivery timelines all the time. One solution to this problem is to consider using apps and programs that can help stream-line the delivery process. We discussed quite a number of emerging technologies in Chapter 6 that can help with this.

The innovations we need aren't limited to timely deliveries. As a trucker, it's important that you run a responsible business that cares for the environment. We all know the huge environmental crisis we are facing at the moment. Climate change is upon us, and we all have a role to play in making sure that future generations have a safe and healthy environment. How can we improve air quality while driving all over the nation in our trucks? Electric vehicles have been a hit in the con-sumer auto markets. We can learn from that, and speed up the adoption of similar vehicles in the trucking and transportation industry.

We are surrounded by lots of new and emerging technologies that are bound to be game-changers. Take the case of driver shortages, for example. Several solutions have been fronted in the past, including retaining drivers by offering better wages, benefits, and offering new drivers training on crucial issues like route planning, optimizing routes to improve overall driver productivity, and making plans to predict and solve disruptions in the distribution channels. These suggestions, when implemented alongside specific technologies, have the potential to help in overcoming the driver shortage crisis and addressing other issues that may affect the drivers' productivity.

Even though so much has been said of the pandemic's impact, the trucking sector was already struggling with a shortage of qualified drivers before 2020. The average age for qualified and experienced truck drivers is 50 years. This means that most of this experience will be retiring soon. Unfortunately, the next generation of drivers, the millennials, are not taking up truck driving as much as the industry's needs require. Gone are the days when trucking was a generational heritage, when kids would grow up hoping to follow in the footsteps of their trucker parents or grandparents.

Most people consider compensation as a major factor in the decision to become truck drivers. Beyond that, there's also the issue of the trucker lifestyle that you have to think about. To retain some of the best drivers in the industry, we must also consider route preferences, the kind of equipment the driver will be working with, proximity to their homes, and the amount of time they can spend at home. This calls for a lot of planning and scheduling, which could easily be achieved with innovative tech solutions.

Walmart, for example, hired more than 14,000 truck drivers to streamline their supply chain. However, sustained growth in sales means that they'll still need more skilled truck drivers to ensure their sales growth does not outpace their delivery efforts. To attract qualified truckers, the retail giant increased their average truck driver salaries to $87,500, which is almost double the industry average ($44,500). Other benefits Walmart drivers get include having two days off every week and three weeks of paid annual leave. Such benefits make it easier to attract and retain experienced truck drivers.

## Intermodal Truck Efficiency

As the demand for efficient delivery increases, so does the pressure on trucking businesses to seek sustainable, economical, and efficient solutions. Intermodal transportation is one of the solutions that many truckers have employed in the past, and it will become even more prevalent in the future.

Intermodal involves moving cargo through two or more forms of transportation, for example, a truck plus rail, or truck plus rail and ocean. Truckers who employ this model mostly use stackable containers that can be moved freely without reloading or repackaging the shipment. The need for intermodal transport comes from the fact that independent over the road (OTR) transportation is becoming too expensive, and may be unsustainable in the future. OTR is often plagued with environmental concerns, insufficient capacity, and unstable fuel costs, among other issues, which make it difficult for trucking companies to run profitable ventures. This is where intermodal transport comes in—cost-effective, and good for the environment.

The fact that cargo isn't handled while it's moved from one mode of transportation to another (could even be from one truck to another) means that you'll save on handling costs. Intermodal transportation is cost-effective if you are moving freight across long distances. To limit cargo handling, cargo is sealed as cargo transport units, mostly as semi-trailers, mobile boxes, or containers. This also reduces other handling problems like theft, breakage, or loss.

The point of intermodality is to encourage better use of resources across different modes of transportation, making the transition of cargo from one point to the next more efficient and cost-effective. For customers, intermodal transport makes sense if your shipment can't fill an entire container. This is because your shipment could be consolidated with other customers' shipments that are heading to the same destination, and eventually fill an entire container.

On logistics, intermodal will save you a lot of time because of the limited handling involved. Unless you fill an entire container with your shipment, handling is usually a logistical nightmare. Intermodal transport helps you overcome this problem. Since your cargo won't be separated, it's easier to track it even when the load is transferred to a different truck. Besides, the fact that your cargo is sealed means that it can only be opened once it arrives at the intended destination.

Another logistical concern that many shippers have is dealing with customs. Since your cargo is sealed, you should have an easier time with inspections, controls, and other customs procedures. A faster, more efficient customs clearing process allows you more time on your delivery schedule, making it even easier to optimize final delivery to your customers.

Environmentally, intermodal efficiency is one of the trucking industry's contributions to the conservation and preservation agenda. Since the cargo is packed once and only unpacked upon final delivery, your energy consumption for every unit of cargo transported is considerably lower than using the normal transportation approach. Intermodal is also a more sustainable method with a smaller carbon footprint because most of the points of inefficiency that usually result in carbon emissions are limited through reduced handling.

In summary, as you are building a transportation and trucking business that will be profitable, sustainable, and viable into the future, you should strongly consider working intermodal transportation into your business model. This will help you maximize your trucking efficiency, cost-effective services, and for your customers, punctuality and flexible delivery schedules.

## Automation and the Trucking Industry

It's hard to talk about the future of any industry without diving into automation. Taking the example of the past decade, automation and modern-day technologies have given many sectors the cutting edge to innovate and become more efficient, and this trend will only continue into the future. The trucking and transportation industry is no different either. Following in the footsteps of the wider auto industry in general, automation is the next big thing for trucking.

The supply chain has struggled to handle the pressure of increasing consumer demand for many years. On their part, consumers have generally pushed the limits of automation in their lives, finding different ways of integrating gadgets and programs. It's all about making life easier, more comfortable, and more efficient. Therefore, it's only fair that the trucking sector adapts to meet this growing demand.

With advancements like the Internet of Things (IoT), artificial intelligence, machine learning, and advanced analytics, we have already seen glimpses of how much we can improve our lives through automation. Therefore, it's vital that the trucking and transportation sector gets on board to run their businesses with ease by using technology to improve efficiency and delivery timelines along supply chains.

Truckers, for example, struggle with safety risks and health problems because they spend extremely long hours on the road. This increases the risk of accidents and delivery delays. When that happens, a chain of events is set in motion, and the effect may be increased costs for everyone involved, up to the final customer. To counter these issues, some big brands, like Amazon, have invested heavily in self-driving trucks.

It was always going to be just a matter of time until these trucks got into the trucking business. So far, we already have self-driving cars that are being perfected, and even though some may or may not be on the road yet, we trust that they can help us commute safely. You get the feeling that this would be a good time to introduce the same concept to trucks. While this sounds like a brilliant idea, it comes with unique challenges. For example, wholesale deployment of self-driving trucks may be decades away, yet we already know it may result in job losses. Think about it for a moment: an automated truck would save you on most, if not all, personal costs associated with having a driver.

However, remember that we had earlier highlighted how the trucking and transportation sector is a networking industry. Drivers talk to other drivers, company owners, and so on. Networking helps you stay informed about what's happening on the road, and what other companies are doing for their drivers. An automated truck will most certainly deny you such benefits. All you know is that your truck will move from one point to the next, and probably track its position throughout the journey. That's about all the communication or information you'll get once the truck is on the road. So, as much as there's a lot of hype and excitement around automated trucks, there are many moving parts that must align for this concept to be fully accepted and implemented throughout the industry.

The fact remains that even with more automation, and self-driving trucks coming into the industry, the trucking business is largely a human-intensive sector. You still need people to get a lot of things going the right way, so at best, we can anticipate a hybrid environment where technological advances are gradually introduced into the trucking workforce to improve efficiency.

## The Impact of Online Shopping

Online shopping is one sector that has propelled the need for accelerated growth in the trucking industry. Consumer demand has been on a steady rise over the years, a trend that will continue in the future. This means that the existing trucking infrastructure must adapt to address this demand, and avoid a supply chain crisis.

Customers generally demand prompt delivery. This is one of the platforms on which retail giants like Amazon have built their success. As a customer, it feels good to know that you can order something online from overseas and have it delivered to your doorstep in a few days. There was a time when next-day delivery was a key selling point across e-commerce platforms. We've outgrown that, and today, same-day delivery is the real deal. Clearly, truckers who can adapt and evolve alongside the changing consumer needs will have a lot of opportunities.

Naturally, the growth of e-commerce, especially during the holidays or seasonal shopping periods when many retailers offer sales, has resulted in booming business for truckers. Short trips—for example, delivery within neighborhoods—have increased. The good news for truckers here is that such trips allow you the freedom to spend time with your family, as opposed to being on the road for days. If you are worried about work-life balance, deliveries for online shoppers may be a good place to start.

Large companies whose supply chains are relatively more complex than most, like Amazon, will try to meet their growing customer needs by investing in advanced technology for their trucks. After all, they have already figured out how to manage customer expectations while still meeting customer needs as well as achieving the financial goals and business objectives of their company. The next step would be complementing this with innovative approaches to product delivery.

Another important lesson about e-commerce is that people love convenience. We recently experienced how much this is true during the global Covid pandemic. Instead of stepping out, most people preferred ordering whatever they could online and having it delivered to their doorsteps. As we get used to the post-pandemic world, it's fair to note that many people have stuck to this shopping approach.

As our shopping habits change over the years, so will the need for the transportation and trucking industry in order to meet our shopping needs.

## Women in Trucking

Trucking culture has changed gradually over the years. This is an industry that was traditionally a man's job. Today, however, not only are women getting into the trucking business, but many of them are enjoying massive success as well. Over the years, female truck drivers have pushed beyond the limits of traditional industries in a bid to get their voices heard, and also prove that the world is changing. Their input is just as important as their male counterparts' input, and they make an impact in any industry.

While most of the attention in this dynamic shift focuses on the female drivers behind the wheels, that's not the limit of women's contribution to this industry. We have CEOs, managers, accountants, and many other professional roles that are currently held by women. Many are running successful trucking enterprises. More young female drivers are applying for different positions in the trucking industry, and that's a good thing because it helps to break down the stereotypes that have sustained inequalities in the trucking industry for many years.

One of the reasons why the industry needs to be more accessible for women is to help address the driver shortage. For as long as we can remember, the driver shortage has always been a problem in this industry. Therefore, it makes a lot of sense that making the industry conducive for women will actually help address this problem. Today, as long as you have your CDL and are interested in becoming a trucker, investor, owner-operator, or part of the CDL Industry, you should be good to go.

There are currently lots of initiatives that are aimed at making the industry more conducive to women truckers. You'll find training programs that teach new female truckers important lessons on trucking, and life on the road. Other supportive initiatives include encouraging social circles for women, which are great for learning, growth, and support. Gender inclusivity in the trucking business is a process that doesn't end at accepting women into the business. There's also room for policy and procedural reforms that will affect the industry for generations to come.

## Technology: The Benefits and Burdens

Even though there's a lot of cutting-edge technology around us, and it's a good thing, implementing it isn't always as smooth as we'd wish. While we mostly recognize the successful technological implementations in trucking, we must also be alert to the potential challenges involved in using some of these programs.

There's been a lot of talk about electronic trucks and autonomous trucks, as the trucking industry tries to catch up with the rest of the automobile world on futuristic approaches to make the industry more efficient. So far, this hasn't fully taken off yet, and such futuristic trucks are mostly still a niche concept.

There are different kinds of sensors that are fitted on trucks, for example, adaptive cruise control, optical cameras, and collision avoidance systems. These sensors monitor the performance of brakes, tires, and other parts of the truck, providing useful information to drivers while on the road, and to your management team on things like scheduling maintenance and regular servicing.

While these technologies have been mostly useful, drivers are usually hesitant to use some of them. For example, in-cab cameras are helpful when assessing insurance claims in the event of an accident. On the other hand, some drivers feel their employers use this to spy on them.

One of the most controversial technologies so far has been the electronic logging device mandated by the government. This monitors the truck's engine performance on the road, and is meant to prevent the issue of overworking drivers. By federal law, drivers must not drive more than 11 hours in a 14-hour window day. These hours are subject to change over a period of time by federal law, so be sure to keep yourself updated on the hours of service that a driver is allowed. Exceeding these limits may earn you a fine, or a federal violation.

For drivers who are used to long-haul trucking, this approach denies them the freedom to manage their time. The time limits imposed also mean that they can no longer reach their personal trucking limits as they used to before. The worst thing about it is that while these technologies mostly aim to improve efficiency and safety standards by targeting trucks and drivers, they haven't done much in terms of the hours drivers must wait for loading or delivery appointments, which are wasted hours. Most drivers are only paid for the number of miles they drive, so the wait times are a loss to drivers.

As we discussed in Chapter 6, there are lots of trucking technologies that have been widely adopted throughout the industry. These are simple but effective gadgets, programs, and apps that help drivers make better decisions on the road, and monitor the overall performance of their trucks. Overall, these help to improve the safety of the road and address one of the industry's biggest challenges since the beginning of time—losing control of the truck.

## Checklist and CDL Minded Approach

One of the smartest things you can do for your business is to set it up for continuity and sustainability. This means building a trucking business that can adapt to evolving times, customer needs, technologies, and business processes. Use this checklist to focus on building a successful future-proof business:

| Activity | What to look for | Complete? Yes or No |
|---|---|---|
| Innovation | Continually research market and industry trends to understand what's going on, and the impact of technology on your business and the industry at large. This should help you prepare for impending changes. | |
| Efficiency | Find out ways you can improve your business and customer experiences by making your trucking service more efficient. Improved delivery timelines, and intermodal trucking are some ideas you should consider. | |

| Get with the trends | More people are shopping on-line today, not just for clothes and shoes, but for pretty much everything. Find out how to set up your business to align with customer needs in the delivery business. | |
| Inclusivity | Strive to make your trucking business as inclusive as possible. Do more than just make your trucking business women-friendly; break the stereotypes. Make your business conducive for disabled people and any other groups that are often disadvantaged in many industries. | |

# CONCLUSION

All businesses rely on trucking and transportation in different capacities. This is why this industry is often considered the backbone of our economy. In fact, truckers are also the glue that holds international trade together. Think about it for a moment—without truckers, how would products arrive at seaports, airports, and railway stations? How would they even leave factories?

Truckers don't just connect people and businesses with goods, they also ensure that products are delivered on time, which is crucial for individuals and enterprises to meet their business goals. Planes, ships, and trains may transport cargo all over the world, but the trucking industry still handles more cargo than they do. If anything, none of these industries would thrive or even survive without trucks. Trucking is so important that if the industry collapsed, the entire economy would suffer.

On paper, it may seem simple enough to start making money from trucking, and even establish a successful business, billing customers to pick up and deliver freight. However, once you get into the driver's seat, you soon realize that there's more to it. You have to put in long hard hours at times, just to make sure that everything works out. At the back of your mind, you know that your success depends on keeping your customers satisfied. This means timely pickup and delivery, consistent communication, and updates throughout the delivery process. Yet, that's just a fraction of the job.

Running a successful transportation and trucking business also means that there are times when you'll be looking for drivers as much as you are looking for freight to deliver. As you do all this, you must also ensure that your operational costs don't overtake your profits. There are lots of people who've been driven out of the industry, especially first-timers, simply because they were unable to keep their costs under control. This is proof that it takes more than just your knowledge of trucks and trucking operations to succeed in this industry. You must also have the business mindset for it.

Having the right mindset for success is often the difference between success and failure in the trucking business. We addressed this at the beginning of the book to prepare you psychologically. Your perception of the challenges you encounter while running the business will play a huge role in your success. For example, some people may be disappointed and feel like giving up when things don't go their way, and probably quit the business altogether. On the other hand, some people treat misfortunes as vital life lessons, and by learning from them, as a stepping stone toward their success.

The overall nature of the trucking industry is such that there are always several moving parts, so you won't always be able to control every aspect of your business. The secret is in how to manage the factors you can control, and how to prepare and respond, or react accordingly to those that you cannot control. For example, you can't control traffic jams. However, we discussed some technological advances that can help your drivers figure out better routes that avoid congestion on the roads. You must learn to be proactive.

Another important lesson about the CDL trucking and transportation business is that your work doesn't start and end with trucks. Since you are running a business, you must also plan for other business roles that will be as crucial to your success as having the right trucks. In this case, we are talking about business roles like customer service, clerical work, bookkeeping, and accounting. These are mostly known as back-office operations.

Even though your drivers do the physical work of moving cargo from one point to the next, they don't get to interact with your customers directly, you should have a separate team for that. You will also need an accountant to help you figure out your finances and more importantly, your taxes. You don't want a run-in with the IRS.

One of the most important things your trucking business needs to thrive is your networking ability. Trucking is an interesting industry where your network will almost always guarantee you jobs round the clock. Go for those networking gigs, and reach out to other truckers who have been in the business for years. The lessons you learn through this, and the contacts you gain, will be invaluable to your business.

While the topics we've discussed in this book will go a long way in helping you run a successful trucking business, it's hard to go all the way without discipline. Discipline is one of the most important skills yet no one will actually sit you down and teach you. It's a valuable skill you have to learn and master on your own. Remember that it's a highly competitive industry, and even bigger, more experienced trucking companies have failed before for lack of discipline. Managing the financial and logistical aspects of your business, in particular, requires a lot of discipline. Without proper management, you can easily run the business into the ground by struggling with rising costs. The competition never sleeps either, so if your business is failing, there'll always be other trucking companies ready to swoop in and serve your customers.

It's not all doom and gloom, though. The trucking business is one of the essential service sectors that have thrived despite pandemics, economic crises, environmental challenges, and advancing technology. We can expect this industry to continue thriving and providing more opportunities for new and existing truckers alike. If you are ready to put in the work, you will reap massive benefits from the trucking sector.

Trucking is one of the very few business opportunities that allow you to make a lot of money within your first year of operation. With the right training, guidance, and information, all you need is that CDL and the right approaches, and you'll be on your way to establishing your trucking empire. You don't necessarily have to start big to become big in the industry. Everyone who's done it started with one step at a time, and you can do it too. Even better, this guide helps you overcome most of the mistakes that many first-time truckers make, so you can keep moving forward and focus on building your trucking empire one mile at a time.

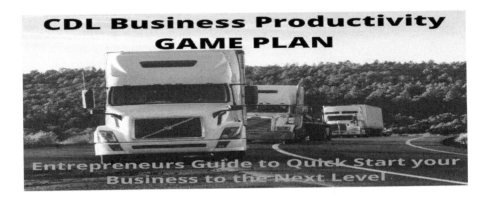

Thank you! Here's a Free Gift! For You :)

As a special thanks from me to you, you'll receive:

- ❑ 3 Powerful Elements of Productivity in your Business
- ❑ 5 Simple Strategies to Mastering Productivity in your Business
- ❑ The Highest Quality of Productivity Charts
- ❑ Valuable Resources that you Must Know and much more!

To receive your Free copy of the CDL Business Productivity GAME PLAN, you can go to my website at:

cdlforlife.com/cdl-business-resources

<u>SCAN ME</u>
(For your Free Business Game Plan)

<u>SCAN ME</u>
(If you want my Books for Free)

Also If you would like to get my books for Free and before anyone else, go to my website at:

cdlforlife.com/cdl-business-resources

# GLOSSARY

Axle Rating—Maximum weight allowed on an axle or a set of axles

Backhaul—A trip that returns the driver back home, or closer home.

Bill of Lading—A document that confirms an agreement between the carrier and shipper, and must be signed by both parties to be effective.

Bulk Freight—This is cargo that generally travels in large volumes but is never packaged, for example, gasoline and sand.

Cargo Insurance—Insurance cover protecting the freight against any damage or loss while in transit.

Cargo Manifest—A list of all the cargo in the truck.

Carrier—Owner-operator or trucking company that transports cargo for shippers.

Carrier Liability—This is the highest possible amount a carrier will be liable for in the event of delivery delays, loss, or damage while the cargo is in transit.

Commercial Learner's Permit (CLP)—This permit is issued once you pass the written section of the CDL test. With the CLP, you can drive a commercial truck, but only if supervised by a CDL holder.

Compliance Review—Set of requirements by the FMCSA to ascertain whether all carriers follow the set safety regulations. Ex: A safety inspection.

Consignee—The company or individual to whom the delivery will be made, also known as a receiver.

Consignor—The company or individual sending the cargo.

Consolidation—A process of combining several less-than-truckload (LTL) cargoes into one big shipment, ending up with a full truckload (FTL).

Contract Carrier—A carrier contracted to offer transportation services to a shipper regularly.

Certified Public Accountant (CPA)—A professional who through education, licensing and experience, can provide accounting advisory services to customers. Note that the CPA title is issued by the Board of Accountancy in every state, and is only provided to licensed accounting professionals.

Declared Value—This is the total value of the cargo as declared by the owner or the shipper.

Demurrage—Also known as detention, it is the carrier's compensation for using their equipment or time in excess of what was contractually agreed. The excess claim may also arise out of loading and unloading delays.

Dispatcher—A coordinator working with a trucking company or carrier to manage back-office activities, and also acts as the link between shippers and drivers to coordinate loads.

Daily Log—An elaborate record of the driver's workday, including their off-duty hours.

Drop & Hook—A situation where the driver delivers an empty trailer at the loading dock, and leaves with a pre-loaded one. This process reduces the wait time for drivers.

Dunnage—Foam padding, lumber, inflatable bags or any other material used to fill the empty space in a truck and prevent cargo from falling or smashing against the sides of the truck.

Endorsements—A special addition to your CDL that allows you to haul or drive special vehicles like hazardous materials or a tanker that's not usually in your job description.

Enrolled Agent (EA)—A federally authorized tax professional who can represent you, the taxpayer, before the IRS for any tax issue like an appeal, collections, or an audit. To qualify for this role, the enrolled agent must have either gained experience as a former employee of the IRS, or passed the comprehensive test set by the IRS, covering business and individual tax returns.

Financial Advisor—A financial advisor is a professional who offers financial guidance to customers on matters like tax planning, investment management, insurance, retirement, and so on. Most financial advisors can handle almost every aspect of your financial life.

Fingerprint a load—This is a unique request specifying that the driver must personally unload the cargo at its destination.

Freight invoice—Also known as freight bill, is the final bill carriers send shippers for the services rendered. As the updated and final bill, it includes any additional expenses that may not have been in the original bill.

Hazardous Materials (Hazmat)—Federally controlled materials that may be dangerous or toxic can only be transported with hazmat CDL endorsement.

Hot Load—Cargo that must be transported and delivered as fast as possible.

Hours of Service (HOS) Regulations—These indicate the total number of hours you can be on duty before you take a mandatory break.

Icing Charge—An additional charge for adding ice to perishable, time-sensitive cargo to keep it fresh, either during the trip or before you begin the trip.

In Bond—Cargo that is yet to be cleared by customs either for import or export.

Interchange Agreement—A common arrangement along border towns where two carriers agree to exchange pickup and delivery cargo. This way, they avoid making the return trip empty.

Less-than-Truckload (LTL)—This represents a situation where the cargo quantity isn't sufficient to fill an entire truckload rate. To make things easier and more affordable for both the carrier and shipper, most shippers organize and consolidate different LTL cargo into an FTL.

Motor Carrier Number (MC Number)—Carrier license issued by the FMCSA.

Onboard Computer—A computer installed in trucks to collect information on crucial points like speed, truck location, fuel consumption, and so on.

Oversized Load—A load whose size is larger than the standard freight size the truck is licensed to carry. You must obtain a permit to haul such a load, and have an escort throughout the journey.

Owner-Operator—This is a situation where you own your truck, and you either get freight from load boards, or have a contract with a carrier. This is one of the highest-paying positions in the trucking business, but it also requires you to invest a lot of your time and resources into building your profile and growing your network.

P&D—Pickup and delivery.

Partial—Combining multiple customer cargoes into one truck to maximize its full carrying capacity. Note that because of multiple off-loading at different destinations, these shipments generally take longer to deliver.

Proof of Delivery (POD)—Official documentation confirming that a shipment is delivered. It must be signed and stamped by the recipient.

Restriction—A restriction is the opposite of an endorsement. It is meant to limit the type of trucks you can operate, or how you drive. For example, an air brakes restriction means that you cannot drive a truck that uses air brakes.

Shipping Order—Document from the shipper to the carrier, confirming that the cargo has been scheduled and booked.

Trans-Load—This is a situation where cargo is moved from one truck to another to proceed with the delivery, especially across international borders. It is common where a carrier's permit only allows them to operate in one of the two countries, not both.

Waybill—This document is provided by the carrier, listing all the important information concerning the shipment.

# REFERENCES

Amblard, M. (2020, March 26). *The future of truck-ing*. Medium; The Startup. https://medium.com/swlh/the-future-of-trucking-7b8208e7a29f

American Trucking Associations. (2020). *Economics and industry data*. American Trucking Associations. https://www.trucking.org/economics-and-industry-data

AMG Funds. (2014). *The effect of compounding*. Amgfunds.com. https://www.amgfunds.com/research_and_insights/investment_essentials/practical/the-effect-of-compounding.html

ATBS Staff. (2020, September 14). *5 Questions a CPA must know about owner-operator taxes*. ATBS. https://www.atbs.com/post/owner-operator-tax-questions-a-cpa-must-know

Bates, L. (2021, January 8). *Using the wealth formula to boost investment success*. MoneySense. https://www.moneysense.ca/save/investing/using-the-wealth-formula-to-boost-investment-success/

Bates, L. (2021, February 19). *7 Questions to ask your financial advisor*. MoneySense. https://www.moneysense.ca/save/investing/7-questions-to-ask-your-financial-advisor/

Bates, L. (2021, April 8). *How to cultivate the right mindset for investing success.* MoneySense. https://www.moneysense.ca/save/investing/how-to-cultivate-the-right-mindset-for-investing-success/

Bobit, B. (2021, August 19). *6 essential tips to master trucking bookkeeping.* Solution Scout. https://solutionscout.com/bookkeeping-services/trucking-bookkeeping/

Business Insider India. (2019, June 3). *11 incredible facts about the $700 billion US trucking industry.* Business Insider India. https://www.businessinsider.in/slideshows/miscellaneous/11-incredible-facts-about-the-700-billion-us-trucking-industry/slidelist/69635128.cms

Commercial Fleet Financing. (2020, July 17). *Invest in the right equipment that will make you the most money.* Commercial Fleet Financing. https://commercialfleetfinancing.com/the-equipment-that-will-make-you-money-f20/

Das, P. (2020, January 17). *4 ways tech can improve your investment strategy.* Entrepreneur. https://www.entrepreneur.com/article/344891

Davis, L. M. (2021, December 30). *Trucking in America: everything you bought in 2021 moved on a truck.* CNET. https://www.cnet.com/tech/tech-industry/features/trucking-in-america-everything-you-bought-in-2021-moved-on-a-truck/

eCapital. (2020, October 21). *How do trucking companies make good money?* eCapital. https://ecapital.com/en-ca/blog/how-do-trucking-companies-make-good-money/

Edema, R. (2022). *The mindset of a winner: How to think like a champion.* RoliEdema.com. https://www.roliedema.com/mindset-of-a-winner.html

ET Money. (2021, December 10). *How even low risk investments can give you high returns.* ET Money Blog. https://www.etmoney.com/blog/how-even-low-risk-investments-can-give-high-returns/

Expensivity. (2020, July 29). *10 biggest mistakes beginner investors make.* Expensivity. https://www.expensivity.com/biggest-mistakes-beginner-investors

Forrest. (2021, December 7). *30+ ways to make money with a truck (complete 2022 guide).* Don't Work Another Day | Personal Finance & Investing Blog. https://www.dontworkanotherday.com/how-to-make-money-with-a-truck

Friedman, D. (2021, November 6). *20 legit ways to make money with a truck - start a new side hustle!* This online world. https://thisonlineworld.com/make-money-with-truck

Furhmann, R. (2021, October 20). *How the internet has changed investing.* Investopedia. https://www.investopedia.com/financial-edge/0212/how-the-internet-has-changed-investing.aspx

Groww. (2021, August 13). *5 common stock investing mistakes to avoid as a beginner.* Groww. https://groww.in/blog/common-stock-investing-mistakes-to-avoid-as-a-beginner

Indeed Editorial Team. (2022, February 23). *15 tips for goal setting.* Indeed Career Guide. https://www.indeed.com/career-advice/career-development/goal-setting-tips

Investopedia Team. (2022, March 21). *Determining risk and the risk pyramid*. Investopedia. https://www.investopedia.com/articles/basics/03/050203.asp

Jones, C. (2021, November 8). *Three ways truck technology can tackle seasonal challenges, driver shortages*. Fleetequipmentmag.com. https://www.fleetequipmentmag.com/three-ways-truck-technology/

Klimashousky, D. (2022, April 30). *Making an investment plan for you in 5 steps*. SmartAsset. https://smartasset.com/investing/how-to-make-an-investment-plan

Lehner Investments. (2020, January 30). *What is a good investment? – Traits of a good investment opportunity for long-term success as investor*. Lehner Investments. https://www.lehnerinvestments.com/en/traits-of-good-investment-opportunity-long-term-success/

Lemke, T. (2022, March 21). *Good investment*. The Balance. https://www.thebalance.com/what-is-a-good-investment-2388572

Litwin, D. (2021, August 2). *Keep on truckin': the future of the trucking industry*. MarketScale. https://marketscale.com/industries/transportation/keep-on-truckin-the-future-of-the-trucking-industry/

Logistics Plus. (2021, November 17). *Trucking equipment types – logistics plus*. Logistics Plus. https://www.logisticsplus.com/services/ship-truckload-more/equipment-types/

Marcom, H. (2017, March 6). *Is the trucking business profitable?* Apex Capital. https://www.apexcapitalcorp.com/blog/is-the-trucking-business-profitable/

Marsh, A. (2017, December 20). *7 truck technologies you need (and why)*. FleetOwner. https://www.fleetowner.com/technology/article/21701619/7-truck-technologies-you-need-and-why

Mathews, B. (2019, April 17). *The impact of technology on trucking – inbound logistics*. Inboundlogistics.com. https://www.inboundlogistics.com/cms/article/the-impact-of-technology-on-trucking/

Mind Tools®. (2017). *Golden rules of goal setting: Five rules to set yourself up for success*. Mindtools.com. https://www.mindtools.com/pages/article/newHTE_90.htm

Mistretta, A. (2017, November 25). *18 ways technology has changed investing*. Stacker. https://stacker.com/stories/205/18-ways-technology-has-changed-investing

Mortson, M. (2022, April 7). *How trucking companies make money!* Supply Chain Game Changer™. https://supplychain-gamechanger.com/how-trucking-companies-make-money/

Motola, C. (2021, May 18). *What is equipment financing & how does it work?* Merchant Maverick. https://www.merchantmaverick.com/equipment-financing/

Muchira, M. (2017, September 26). *How to start a trucking business in Texas*. Bizfluent. https://bizfluent.com/how-6906378-start-trucking-business-texas.html

Newlands, M. (2022). *How to tell when an investment isn't working out*. Incafrica.com. https://incafrica.com/library/murray-newlands-the-5-signs-of-failure-how-to-tell-when-an-investment-isn-t-working-out

Newton, E. (2022, April 1). *Fixing the truck driver shortage.* The Network Effect. https://supplychainbeyond.com/how-technology-can-alleviate-the-truck-driver-shortage/

Palmer, B. (2022, February 24). *How to invest on a shoestring budget.* Investopedia. https://www.investopedia.com/articles/younginvestors/07/shoestring_budget.asp#toc-other-considerations

Pham, M. (2022, March 25). *How much does it cost to start your trucking business?* Motive (Formerly KeepTruckin). https://gomotive.com/blog/cost-starting-trucking-business/

Picardo, E. (2021, August 18). *Common investor and trader blunders.* Investopedia. https://www.investopedia.com/articles/active-trading/013015/worst-mistakes-beginner-traders-make.asp

Placek, M. (2022, April 20). *Trucking industry in the U.S.* Statista. https://www.statista.com/topics/4912/trucking-industry-in-the-us/#dossierKeyfigures

Rasmussen, R. (2021, May 21). *Is the trucking business profitable? Challenges and opportunities.* Fast Capital 360. https://www.fastcapital360.com/blog/is-the-trucking-business-profitable/

Rasmussen, R. (2021, August 16). *12 top trucking technologies that can give you a competitive edge.* Fast Capital 360. https://www.fastcapital360.com/blog/trucking-technology-you-need/

Ryan, E. (2022, April 28). *Equipment financing.* Fast Capital 360. https://www.fastcapital360.com/business-loans/business-equipment-financing/

Sablan, T. (2020, April 27). *Get Into The Right Investing Mindset By Asking These Five Questions.* Forbes. https://www.forbes.com/sites/forbesfinancecouncil/2020/04/27/get-into-the-right-investing-mindset-by-asking-these-five-questions

Sharetown. (2022, February 18). *How to make money with a truck [10 ways].* Sharetown. https://sharetown.com/blog/make-money-with-truck/

Simpson, S. D. (2021, August 18). *Low-risk vs. High-risk investments: What's the difference?* Investopedia. https://www.investopedia.com/financial-edge/0512/low-vs.-high-risk-investments-for-beginners.aspx

Siragusa, T. (2020, March 17). *The importance of developing a winning mindset.* Medium; Radical Purpose. https://medium.com/radical-culture/the-importance-of-developing-a-winning-mindset-cf3aec8f47d

Smith Schafer & Associates LTD. (2019, July 11). *Why do you need a CPA specialized in the transportation industry?* Smith Schafer & Associates. https://www.smithschafer.com/blog/why-do-you-need-a-cpa-specialized-in-the-transportation-industry/

Tobias Financial. (2019, February 22). *What are the advantages of a CPA financial advisor?* Www.tobiasfinancial.com. https://tobias-financial.com/2019/02/22/what-are-the-advantages-of-a-cpa-financial-advisor/

Truck Writers. (2016, May 4). *Becoming an owner operator: Trucking equipment.* Truck Writers. https://www.truckwriters.com/blog/trucking-equipment/

Truckadium. (2020, August 7). *Truckadium – importance of technology in the trucking industry*. Truckadium.com. https://truckadium. com/blog/importance-of-technology-in-trucking-industry

Truckstop. (2021, November 8). *How to start a successful trucking business (14-step checklist)*. Truckstop.com. https://truckstop.com/blog/ 10-steps-to-start-a-successful-trucking-business/

TXP Capital. (2021, September 23). *The benefits of hiring a CPA or bookkeeper for your business*. TXP Capital. https://www.txpcapital. com/financial-insights/the-benefits-of-hiring-a-cpa-or-bookkeeper-for-your-business/

Ward, M. (2017, March 28). *9 habits of highly successful people, from a man who spent 5 years studying them*. CNBC. https://www.cnbc.com/ 2017/03/28/9-habits-of-highly-successful-people.html

Yan, L. (2021, May 3). *Automation is the future of trucking, but it's not all about autonomous driving*. Forbes. https://www.forbes.com/ sites/forbestechcouncil/2021/05/03/automation-is-the-future-of-trucking-but-its-not-all-about-autonomous-driving

Zwahlen, C. (2018, August 28). *5 financial risks every independent trucker should avoid*. Trucks.com. https://www.trucks.com /2018/08/28/5-financial-risks-independent-truckers-avoid/

## Image References

Adams, B. "File:Abnormal Load. Mammoet Mercedes Benz Actros 4161. (16387823332).Jpg - Wikimedia Commons." *Wikimedia.org*, 28 Jan. 2015, commons.wikimedia.org/

wiki/File:Abnormal_Load._Mammoet_Mercedes_Benz_
Actros_4161._(16387823332).jpg. Accessed 8 May 2022.

ArtisticOperations. (2020, June 13). *Dump Truck Truk Jalan.* Pixabay.
com. https://pixabay.com/id/photos/dump-truck-truk-jalan-
dumper-5291994/

ArtisticOperations. (2021, December 5). *Trailer Pengangkut Mobil
Truk.* Pixabay.com. https://pixabay.com/id/photos/trailer-
pengangkut-mobil-truk-jalan-6839728/

ccfb. (2020, February 19). *Keuangan Bank Perbankan.* Pixabay.com.
https://pixabay.com/id/photos/keuangan-bank-perbankan-
bisnis-4858797/

CC0-Photographers. "Free Images : Asphalt, Transport, Hitachi,
Scania, Construction Equipment, Land Vehicle, Trailer Truck,
Low Loader, Five Axes, Narrow Bed 2288x1712." *Pxhere.com,*
2017, pxhere.com/en/photo/1088372. Accessed 8 May 2022.

DigitalGenetics. "3d Render of New City Bus, on White
Background Stock Illustration." *Adobe Stock,* stock.
adobe.com/images/3d-render-of-new-city-bus-on-white-
background/361481314. Accessed 8 May 2022.

ds_30. (2020, January 22). *Muatan Transportasi Truk.* Pixabay.com.
https://pixabay.com/id/photos/muatan-transportasi-truk-
wadah-4783290/

Firmbee. (2015, January 29). *Pembukuan Akuntansi
Pajak.* Pixabay.com. https://pixabay.com/id/photos/
pembukuan-akuntansi-pajak-hunian-615384/

Freedommail. (2018, March 7). *Pelatih Bis Holiday Bus*. Pixabay.com. https://pixabay.com/id/photos/pelatih-bis-holiday-bus-modern-3206326/

geralt. (2016, September 5). *Tanda Nama Tempat Hal Petualangan*. Pixabay.com. https://pixabay.com/id/illustrations/tanda-nama-tempat-hal-petualangan-1647341/

geralt. (2018a, February 3). *Papan Buletin Perekat Post-It*. Pixabay.com. https://pixabay.com/id/photos/papan-buletin-perekat-post-it-3127287/

geralt. (2018b, May 3). *Keterampilan Dapat Rintisan*. Pixabay.com. https://pixabay.com/id/photos/keterampilan-dapat-rintisan-pendiri-3371153/

HiveBoxx. (2020, March 30). *blue and white truck on road during daytime*. Unsplash.com; Unsplash. https://unsplash.com/photos/4GYGZSIto4I

Innovalabs. (2017, October 9). *Pengembang Perangkat Lunak*. Pixabay.com. https://pixabay.com/id/photos/pengembang-perangkat-lunak-6521720/

Mclean, E. (2020, August). *Unrecognizable workman cleaning compartment of cargo tank on city road*. Pexels.com; Pexels. https://www.pexels.com/photo/unrecognizable-workman-cleaning-compartment-of-cargo-tank-on-city-road-4062506/

mohamed_hassan. (2018, September 16). *Daftar Periksa Bisnis Tempat Kerja*. Pixabay.com. https://pixabay.com/id/illustrations/daftar-periksa-bisnis-tempat-kerja-3679741/

Mooney, P. "Flickr." *Flickr*, Scania R500 Refrigerated Trailer - pulls in at Clonard, Co… | Flickr, 12 May 2012, www.flickr.com/photos/peterm7/7182447138. Accessed 8 May 2022.

PublicDomainPictures. (2013, July 19). *Paket Tumpukan Uang*. Pixabay.com. https://pixabay.com/id/illustrations/paket-tumpukan-uang-keuangan-163497/

Ralphs_Fotos. (2019, January 4). *Truk Kendaraan Komersial Mercedes*. Pixabay.com. https://pixabay.com/id/photos/truk-kendaraan-komersial-mercedes-3910170/

rauschenberger. (2020, March 10). *Transportasi Truk Traktor*. Pixabay.com. https://pixabay.com/id/photos/transportasi-truk-traktor-cuplikan-4916922/

raymondclarkeimages. "Flickr." *Flickr*, VERY Long & Heavy Hauler | raymondclarkeimages | Flickr, 5 Sept. 2012, www.flickr.com/photos/rclarkeimages/7958412534/. Accessed 8 May 2022.

richardfoulon. (2021, July 25). *Truk Flatbed Alat Berat*. Pixabay.com. https://pixabay.com/id/photos/truk-truk-flatbed-alat-berat-muatan-6487742/

Winternet. (2020, June 8). *Bus Sekolah Bis Tempat Parkir*. Pixabay.com. https://pixabay.com/id/photos/bus-sekolah-bis-tempat-parkir-3711352/

# Thank you for your Honest Experience :)

Thank you! I hope this brings you great value as it did for me sharing my story with you.

My purpose and mission is to guide and encourage you to become the best version of yourself in your life by providing everything you need to achieve your dreams for yourself, your family and your business.

However, in order to do that, sharing your honest review on **amazon** (or Audible) helps spread the word to other CDL Minded friends (like yourself) and will help many readers who are struggling to make their dreams become a reality.

If you do have 30 seconds to leave a **1-Click honest review,** I greatly appreciate it because it shows that you're not like most people.

It means that you truly value yourself in what you do. It also means that you're CDL Minded in yourself, your family and in your business.

I truly appreciate all your love and support and I'm thankful and grateful for your life and I greatly value your honest opinion and thoughts. :)

If you need anything, feel free to reach out at my website and to receive your Free Gift if you haven't received it yet.

You can also share your experience by taking a photo of this book and attach it to the review so other CDL Minded friends can be inspired and encouraged from your honest experience.

# SCAN ME!

**Just One Click** (once you click on this review page or scan QR Code):

When you finish, just Click Submit at the bottom of the page and that's it. Please click on <u>this link</u> or scan the QR code to **Review Book on Amazon!**

**Overall rating**

☆☆☆☆☆

**Add a headline**

What's most important to know?

**Add a photo or video**

Shoppers find images and videos more helpful than text alone.

+

**Add a written review**

What did you like or dislike? What did you use this product for?

Submit

Looking forward to working together and helping you achieve your goals. Take care and talk to you soon! :)